Chatham
Historic
Dockyard

Chatham Historic Dockyard

World Power to Resurgence

Edited by Neil Cossons

Published by Liverpool University Press on behalf of Historic England, The Engine House, Fire Fly Avenue, Swindon SN2 2EH
www.HistoricEngland.org.uk

Historic England is a Government service championing England's heritage and giving expert, constructive advice.

First published 2021

ISBN: 978-1-80085-949-4 paperback
ISBN: 978-1-80085-617-2 hardback

British Library Cataloguing in Publication data
A CIP catalogue record for this book is available from the British Library.

Neil Cossons has asserted the right to be identified as the editor of this book in accordance with the Copyright, Designs and Patents Act 1988.

Typeset in Charter 9/11

Page layout by Carnegie Book Production

Printed in Czech Republic via Akcent Media Limited.

Front and back cover: View of the Historic Dockyard today. Image reproduced with permission from Chatham Historic Dockyard Trust.

Contents

Acknowledgements

Above all others, Richard Holdsworth deserves fulsome thanks, for without him this book would never have happened. As director of heritage, public engagement and learning at Chatham Historic Dockyard, he managed the relationship with the National Lottery Heritage Fund (NLHF), acted as mentor and adviser to me as editor and, with Victoria Mulford, digital engagement officer, sourced most of the illustrations. Nigel Howard, director of historic environment and buildings, provided many of the photographs of works in progress.

The roots of the idea came about as part of the activity plan for the Trust's most recent major NLHF-funded project. Funded through NLHF's Heritage Enterprise Programme, it saw the Fitted Rigging House, the historic dockyard's last major underutilised building, back into commercial reuse. Bill Ferris, chief executive 2000–20, saw this as a major point in the Trust's journey to financial self-sustainability worth documenting. We owe particular thanks to Eleanor Potter and Lucy Emerson, our NLHF case officers, for their support in this publication and to Liverpool University Press and Historic England for taking the project on.

The majority of illustrations are courtesy of Chatham Historic Dockyard Trust, but a number of historic illustrations have been sourced from institutions to whom we owe thanks: the British Library; the National Gallery; Rijksmuseum, Amsterdam; and Royal Museums Greenwich.

Foreword

His Royal Highness the Prince of Wales
Patron of Chatham Historic Dockyard Trust

CLARENCE HOUSE

As Patron of Chatham Historic Dockyard Trust, and having at one time served in a warship based there during my service in the Royal Navy, it has given me enormous pleasure to see all that has been achieved here over the last forty years. Chatham exemplifies constructive conservation at its best. Dozens of buildings that otherwise might have been lost have been brought back to life for a wide variety of different purposes, according to the principle that a building in use is a building saved. All of this has been achieved without compromising the integrity or quality of this unique historic environment. As a nation, we should feel extremely proud of what has been achieved in this extraordinary historic landscape.

This inspirational conservation programme is only the latest chapter in the yard's remarkable history which stretches back more than four hundred years. In the sixteenth century, it was the Royal Navy's principal base facing the North Sea and it provided a safe haven on the Medway for the fleets protecting the Thames Estuary from threats from the Dutch, while at the same time containing all the facilities necessary to build and maintain sailing warships. By the twentieth century, ships of iron, and later steel, were being built at Chatham and, ultimately, the yard was engaged in the construction of diesel submarines and the refuelling of nuclear-powered vessels.

For four centuries the dockyard had been the largest employer locally, so its closure in 1984 was a profound challenge. However, the community responded with a spirited debate on the future of the site which, by that time, had been recognized as the world's most intact dockyard of the age of sail, with forty-seven of its buildings scheduled as Ancient Monuments, a status which afforded them a degree of protection.

It could all have ended tragically, with the buildings disposed of piecemeal and the priceless architectural unity of the site shattered. Mercifully, thanks to inspired leadership and determined strategic planning, this incomparable historic site was saved and transferred, in its entirety, to a specially-formed Trust. This is the story that is celebrated in this book: the preservation of a landscape that speaks vividly of its history, yet sits gainfully and comfortably in the twenty-first century, and which looks forward confidently to the next four hundred years.

Preface

Admiral Sir Trevor Soar KCB OBE DL
Chairman of the Chatham Historic Dockyard Trust

Sir Trevor Soar.
[Chatham Historic Dockyard Trust]

Chatham Historic Dockyard is a very special place that has had an impact on the lives of many thousands of people over the last 400 years. For me, privileged to be the current chairman of the Trust, it has been an integral part of my own life and career. I joined my first ship here, conducted some of my early training here, brought the first nuclear-powered submarine I served on here for refit, lived in a quarter here when I was first married, and now the dockyard hosts and preserves for all our many visitors my first diesel submarine command HMS *Ocelot*.

Chatham Royal Dockyard has played a crucial role in the history of the Royal Navy and of the nation for over some four centuries. As the major employer in the Medway towns over this period, its significance in the social history of the local community has been incalculable, so closure of the yard in 1984 came as an unprecedented blow.

But one unique quality has proved to be the saviour of the yard and has led over more than 40 years to its growing importance in the regional economy. As this book sets out, Chatham Historic Dockyard offers the most complete evidence of how the sailing navy of wooden warships was built and maintained, an extraordinary testimony to generations of skill and human enterprise. And that endeavour adapted with time from sail to steam, from ships to submarines, and continued through to the nuclear age.

This book for the first time tells in detail the story of the historic dockyard over the last 37 years, from the day this working yard closed to a time where history and heritage are today's drivers of a singular exercise in constructive conservation. Crucial to this has been the work of the Chatham Historic Dockyard Trust, established in 1984 to develop a future for the yard as a place for history, for people and for understanding. I am the sixth chairman of the Trust and I pay enormous tribute to the work of my distinguished predecessors who have brought the yard from dilapidation to its present position of pre-eminence. They have led an outstanding team whose inspiration and expertise we can also celebrate in the pages that follow. In particular, the Trust's chief executive, Bill Ferris, who has led the management team since 2001, supported by Richard Holdsworth, who joined the Trust in 1985, and Nigel Howard, who has equally long associations with the site, all deserve special mention.

I commend this book as a record of outstanding achievement, often against the most challenging odds, to where it is today, 'the most complete dockyard of the age of sail in the world'.

The Chatham endeavour

Neil Cossons

N owhere in the world is it possible to see such a complete and
largely intact naval dockyard for the building and maintenance
of the wooden warships of the sailing navy as at Chatham.
Here is the best preserved of all the Georgian dockyards, its standing
today lying not only in the complete and comprehensive nature of the
surviving evidence, but in the manner that it has been preserved and
managed. At Chatham, good fortune and serendipity, judicious strategic
planning and the very best of professional management have all played
their part, endowing us with a historic site of immense importance and
an international exemplar for what can be achieved given the right
circumstances and the right people in the right place at the right time.
That we have the dockyard today is no accident, although it would be
wrong to assume that its survival after closure was an inevitability. This
book sets out how, from its vital role in the history of the Royal Navy and
of the nation, through closure in the mid-1980s, to the dockyard of today,
Chatham affords us something unique.

The circumstances of Britain's rise as an industrial, imperial and
global power and trading nation put unprecedented and constantly
changing demands upon the Navy. From the early 17th century until the
First World War, those requirements expanded progressively within a
broad public, political and financial consensus that favoured investment
in ships and the infrastructure necessary to keep them at sea. On the
one hand, a relatively small standing army, reflecting deep-seated
domestic concerns about control of the civil population, was contrasted
by an unbounded belief in and commitment to the Royal Navy. Britain's
growing self-assurance was largely founded in this unquestioned
confidence, that her interests, political and commercial, should and
could be protected wherever the need might arise. It was also on the
inferred deterrent of a global naval presence that *Pax Britannica* and
thus the balance of power rested. This climate of faith and conviction,
underwritten by the Navy, encouraged mercantile endeavour and the
investment of private capital both at home and overseas, in merchant
shipping and port facilities and, increasingly, in industrial expansion. This
in turn fuelled a culture of enterprise secure in the knowledge that under
the protective eye of the Navy the nation could see the world as its open
door. As the epicentre of perceived threat moved from the south coast
and the French to the Thames estuary, the Scheldt and the low countries
and back again, so too did investment in the dockyards and their facilities
mirror the nation's requirements.

It is in this context that the history of Chatham Royal Dockyard can
be understood. The scale of the naval enterprise needed extraordinary
facilities, such that by the middle years of the 18th century the Royal
dockyards, and most notably Chatham and Portsmouth, had come to be
the largest industrial enterprises in the world. They were beneficiaries not

View of Chatham Dockyard
commissioned by the Navy Board from
Joseph Farrington. The painting shows the
historic dockyard as it was in 1794.
[National Maritime Museum, Greenwich,
London, Greenwich Hospital Collection]

View of the historic dockyard today
– from a similar perspective as
Farrington's 1794 painting.
[Chatham Historic Dockyard Trust]

Pax Britannica exemplified in
Charles Edward Dixon's painting
In Honour of our Queen: Queen
Victoria's Diamond Jubilee Review at
Spithead 26 June 1897.
[National Maritime Museum,
Greenwich, London,
Caird Collection]

only of the inventive genius that characterised Britain's wider industrial
pre-eminence, but of the changing but critical imperatives demanded
by a trading nation and an emerging global power. What by the 1830s
had come to be called the Industrial Revolution was already signalling a
period of national transformation, widely recognised throughout Europe
and North America. In its earliest, simplest and most domestic sense, new
technologies associated with iron-making and the use of coke instead of
charcoal as a fuel for blast furnaces, the application of steam as a source
of power, innovative engineering technologies, and new manufacturing
techniques were being taken up in the Royal dockyards. Later, the
adoption of iron in, for example, the improvements in ship construction

HMS Royal Oak, a Prince Consort-
class armoured frigate, converted
from wooden-hulled ship to
ironclad while under construction
in No. 3 Dock c 1862.
[Chatham Historic Dockyard Trust]

pioneered by Sir Robert Seppings (1767–1840) and his use of iron for diagonal bracing of wooden hulls, through, ultimately, to iron and later steel for ship construction, all reflected the changing nature of these great industrial installations.

The industrial and technological revolution taking place in the Royal dockyards included new block mills at Portsmouth, installed to satisfy the insatiable demands of the fleet for pulley blocks during the Napoleonic wars. These were some of the first examples of production-line manufacturing and remained in use well into the 20th century. The major industrial addition to Chatham's productivity was the steam-powered sawmills built to designs by Sir Marc Isambard Brunel (1769–1845), which allowed large timber to be sawn down to the sizes suitable for ship construction, quickly and accurately. Previously, gangs of men working in twos – there were over a hundred men so engaged at Chatham – had sawn by hand the enormous volumes of timber needed in the yard. A canal, partly in a tunnel, was used to float the logs from the mast pond to the sawmills. This survives in part today, together with the buildings and part of Brunel's innovative machinery. Paradoxically, as with the block mills at Portsmouth, Chatham and the Navy benefited from the intellect of a French émigré, a Royalist who fled the tyrannies of republican France. Initially he went to the United States, where he became engineer for the City of New York, before arriving in Britain. As engineer for the Thames Tunnel, begun in 1825 and the world's first underwater tunnel, he was assisted by his, ultimately more famous, son, Isambard Kingdom Brunel, himself the designer of three great steamships.

In the following chapters Andrew Lambert and Jonathan Coad, the acknowledged experts on, respectively, the history of the Royal Navy and of the Royal dockyards, plot the history of Chatham and its place in the nation's international positioning, both as deterrent to foes and as part of wider imperial ambitions. It was not until the years after the Second World War that serious questions about the future of all the Royal dockyards reflected a deep and often painful analysis of Britain's role in a post-imperial environment, and the nature and scale of the nation's commitment to NATO during the Cold War years. The inevitable contraction in the size of the Navy meant that the writing was on the wall, most notably at Chatham where shipbuilding had ended in 1968. For generations the largest employer in the Medway towns, the continued presence of the dockyard was taken for granted, so the announcement of closure in June 1981 came not so much as a shock but as something that had long been feared and had to be challenged and contested. But even the post-Falklands euphoria and the obvious stresses that the conflict had placed on the capacity of the Royal Navy were to offer no reprieve.

With closure as a certainty, the debate on the future of the site came into sharp focus. In particular, the historical importance of the Georgian dockyard posed questions for which answers were going to be needed. As early as 1966 Arnold Taylor, chief inspector of ancient monuments in the Directorate of Ancient Monuments and Historic Buildings (DAMHB) in the then Ministry of Public Building and Works, had authorised a wide-ranging assessment of the archaeological and historical assets of the three English naval bases – Chatham, Portsmouth and Devonport. The number and scale of outstanding buildings and dock installations was immense,

November 1981 newsagent poster announcing the dockyard's closure. [Chatham Historic Dockyard Trust]

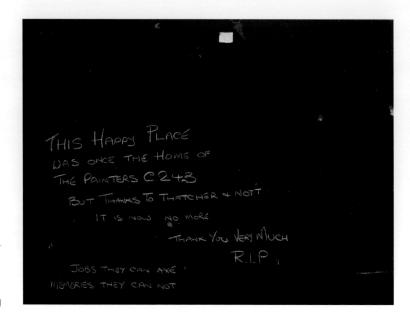

THIS HAPPY PLACE
WAS ONCE THE HOME OF
THE PAINTERS C243
BUT THANKS TO THATCHER & NOTT
IT IS NOW NO MORE
THANK YOU VERY MUCH
R.I.P
JOBS THEY CAN AXE
MEMORIES THEY CAN NOT

'This Happy Place' – message
left on a partition in the Sail and
Colour Loft in 1984.
[Chatham Historic Dockyard Trust]

and in the succeeding years this was reflected in major programmes of scheduling and listing. In 1970 the Ministry of Works had been absorbed into the new Department of the Environment (DoE) and with it the Ancient Monuments Board and the Historic Buildings Council, the main advisory bodies to DAMHB. In 1980, the Ancient Monuments Board, by now strengthened in influence and with strategic ambitions, and in anticipation of threat in the offing, appointed a small panel, chaired by Dr Basil Greenhill, director of the National Maritime Museum at Greenwich, to assess the scale and nature of the heritage assets in the Chatham dockyard. Greenhill's report was unequivocal; Chatham was clearly a site of national importance demanding the utmost care and protection. The critical issue about what to do and how could not have arisen at a more propitious moment.

The initial groundwork for the future of Chatham Historic Dockyard after closure was already well under way in the hands of the local authorities, driven by key people in Kent County Council. The council commissioned a report from leading consultants Richard Ellis, Chartered Surveyors, and Hugh Wilson & Lewis Womersley, Architects & Town Planners. This was published in August 1982 and contained in outline a blueprint for the future of the yard. In one sense the report added little to understanding the importance of the individual historic buildings, such had been the comprehensive analysis of earlier years. But its particular emphasis on holding together the whole historic estate reinforced views that were already emerging locally. The 1982 report also considered in some detail the potential uses for the historic dockyard after closure, concluding that two alternatives merited study in greater detail. One was to make the site into a museum, while the second proposed a 'living dockyard', the precise nature of which had still to be determined, but which envisaged a variety of uses for the dockyard and its buildings, including significant visitor benefit.

Aerial view of the Historic Dockyard at the time of closure. Scaffolding is beginning to be erected at the south end of the Ropery at the start of the £3.3m PSA-let contract, inherited by the Trust, to renew the Ropery roof.

[Chatham Historic Dockyard Trust]

The return of a Conservative administration in 1979 had resulted in a number of cultural and heritage activities then run directly by government coming under scrutiny. One outcome was the National Heritage Act, 1983. Responsibility for departmental museums like the Science Museum and the Victoria & Albert was transferred to boards of trustees, bringing them into line with long-standing trustee-run institutions like the British Museum and the National Gallery. More crucially for Chatham, the state's responsibilities for archaeological and historic sites – there were over 400 open to the public in England alone – and policy advice on listing and scheduling were transferred to a new body, the Historic Buildings and Monuments Commission for England. Vested in April 1984 under the chairmanship of Lord Montagu of Beaulieu, and shortly to be branded English Heritage (now Historic England), the new body set an innovative and more entrepreneurial tone to the care and presentation of the nation's historic properties. All this set the context for debates on the future of the historic dockyard at Chatham.

In short, the closure of Chatham Dockyard, the devolving of the historic estate as a single entity, and its transfer to a trust that would be responsible for future management took place, providentially, at a singular moment in history, one where political circumstances and a newly emerging cultural mood about the care of historic places saw opportunities that would have been unimaginable just a few years earlier. In this, the influence and direct engagement of Michael Heseltine was more than fortuitous. As Environment Secretary from 1979 to 1983 he had already had experience of the transformational prospects afforded by historic estates, most notably on Merseyside. After riots there in the early eighties, his advocacy for a new and visionary approach, as 'Minister for Merseyside', led to the renovation of Albert Dock and, on a broader canvas, the setting up of urban development corporations with budgets and delegated executive powers to get things done. In 1983 Heseltine was appointed Secretary of State for Defence. For Chatham the stage was set.

The options put forward in the August 1982 report made a crucial contribution to the next steps. The proposed museum option was considered very carefully. It would involve the 'development of a national museum, with research and laboratory facilities, using the buildings and sites to trace the history of the Dockyard and the activities and processes that took place there'. The National Maritime Museum was to be a principal participant in this proposal. Here can be seen the influence of the museum's director, Dr Basil Greenhill, who throughout had been most positive and encouraging in the numerous discussions on the future of the yard. Later he became rather more circumspect about the possibility of the proposed museum option, in what might in effect become some sort of merger of the dockyard and the National Maritime Museum, recognising the financial implications not only for the dockyard itself but also for the museum, already running on a very tight budget, and with the move to fixed-budget grant-in-aid funding from government soon to be implemented. However, despite these reservations, he continued to offer enthusiastic encouragement in moves to devise a viable future for the historic yard in which its main elements would be retained and made accessible to the public.

At this time I had for some 12 years been director (CEO) of the Ironbridge Gorge Museum in Shropshire, which was dedicated to preserving this 'Birthplace of the Industrial Revolution'. The analogies with Chatham were seen as more than superficial, and a team from the consultants, as well as – separately – Greenhill himself, visited Ironbridge to test whether it might be a model for the historic dockyard. One essential quality immediately struck a chord with both parties: that the museum, in all its complexity of sites and properties, was governed as a single entity by the board of trustees of a not-for-profit charitable company.

In the summer of 1983 I succeeded Basil as director of the Greenwich Maritime Museum and was promptly drawn into the debate about the future of the historic dockyard at Chatham and especially the setting up of some sort of body to run it. Most of my discussions took place with Harry Deakin, chief planning officer of Kent County Council and a strong advocate for a co-ordinated and strategic approach to the future of the dockyard estate. Central to his thinking was that the historic dockyard should be retained in the ownership and management of a single governing entity. In short, that any temptations to redevelop the site piecemeal or sell off individual properties should be resisted. By this time the consultants had rejected the museum option for the yard's future, recognising the huge amount of capital that would be needed to establish it and the continuing revenue deficit for which there was no obvious source of funding.

Throughout the 1970s new museums and heritage organisations were in the ascendant, opening at an average rate of about one every two weeks. Most were small, but almost without exception they were in what came to be called the 'independent' sector, that is, outside the more traditional format of local or national government funding. Ironbridge was one of the larger examples and the analogy – to the extent that there was one – with Chatham was that it was largely concerned with the preservation *in situ* of listed buildings and ancient monuments, in this case spread across the three miles of the Severn Gorge in Shropshire. Crucially, it was run by a single organisation, the Ironbridge Gorge Museum Trust, a company limited by guarantee and registered as a charity, a not-for-profit body which held the freeholds and leaseholds of the whole estate.

The hunt for convincing role models that might help inform thinking continued, and a small delegation of us visited Lowell in Massachusetts to see the achievements there in revitalising the fortunes of one of the largest historic industrial complexes in the United States. Originally based on the spinning and weaving of cotton, the great Lowell mills had stood empty and largely derelict since the depression years of the late twenties and thirties. Piecemeal rehabbing of individual buildings had not created the step change necessary to revitalise the core area, but a larger, more imaginative and strategic intervention, by a combination jointly of state and federal park services, had proved both effective and transformative in bringing the life, activity and footfall needed to create the critical mass necessary for success. With conservation of Lowell's historic mill buildings as the central thesis, a variety of complementary new uses were developed, notably a museum in the Boott cotton mill and with commercial occupants of other buildings of which, at the time, Wang Laboratories, a pioneer computer company, was an anchor occupant. Here the analogy ended, as the site continued to be run by the United States National Park Service backed by large-scale federal funding.

At Chatham, having rejected the museum option, attention turned to fleshing out the 'living dockyard' concept. The proposal to transfer the freehold and management of the historic yard to a new and purpose-built trust had been accepted in principle and, as Paul Hudson sets out in detail in Chapter 4, there were intense discussions on how this might be achieved in practice, the nature, scale and potential sources of the funding necessary to set the ball rolling, and, crucially, who would form the initial board of trustees. The 'living dockyard' concept was outlined in the 1982 report on the following lines:

> This concept seeks to preserve the historical importance of the Dockyard whilst bringing it to life by incorporating a mix of uses; this might involve adaptation of some of the buildings whilst maintaining their character …

> The general public would be able to appreciate … the historical progress and activities of the Dockyard …

> People would also be encouraged to live and work there.

> We believe and recommend that this approach provides the most realistic opportunities for the preservation of the buildings and character of the Historic Dockyard and will have the best chance to attract private finance.

On this basis, moves went ahead to set up the Chatham Historic Dockyard Trust, the body that since 1984 has run the yard with skill, aplomb and professionalism. Such was the wise and consistent thinking leading to the setting up of the Trust that it has never deviated from its founding objectives, and this is reflected in the prodigious accomplishments of succeeding years. This consistency of policy has been a crucial strength in bringing the historic yard to its current position of pre-eminence. It has also been the foundation upon which critically important funding bodies – most notably the government through the Department for Digital, Culture, Media and Sport [DCMS], Historic England and the National Lottery Heritage Fund – have been committed to supporting a long-term programme of revival of the historic dockyard estate.

Translation of a well-conceived policy into a coherent and workable proposition has been the foundation upon which most of the Trust's activities have continued for nearly 40 years. Richard Holdsworth, who has been a key figure in the development of the dockyard over most of that period, sets out in Chapter 6 a series of case studies that exemplify this judiciously managed approach. Initially work concentrated on adaptation of buildings that required little or no intervention in order to make them suitable for new uses. But, progressively over succeeding years, a more ambitious and innovative approach has emerged enabling more complex adaptations to be implemented, guided throughout by firm leadership from the Trust's chief executive, Bill Ferris, and a robust conservation policy placing a high priority on maintenance of historical and archaeological integrity as a prelude to intelligent adaptation and viable opportunities for reuse. A consistent thread throughout the Trust's work has been a ready willingness, when circumstances change, to think again, regroup around a new agenda, but all the time respecting the core conservation policy criteria. Today, the Trust can be seen as a model guardian of the Royal dockyard, protecting not only the physical estate but the spirit of endeavour that brought it into being.

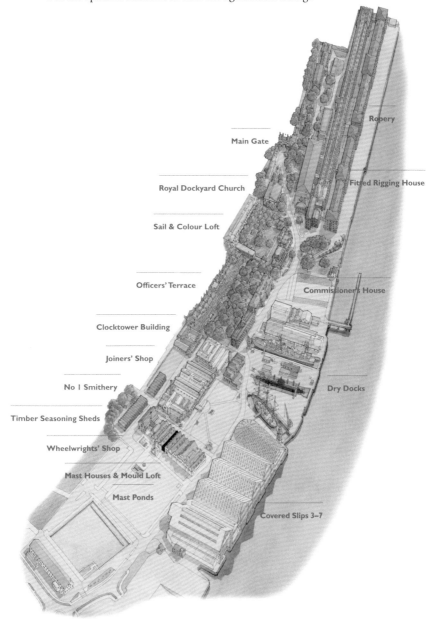

Main Gate

Royal Dockyard Church

Sail & Colour Loft

Officers' Terrace

Clocktower Building

Joiners' Shop

No 1 Smithery

Timber Seasoning Sheds

Wheelwrights' Shop

Mast Houses & Mould Loft

Mast Ponds

Ropery

Fitted Rigging House

Commissioner's House

Dry Docks

Covered Slips 3–7

The historic dockyard today:
Illustrated plan.
[Chatham Historic Dockyard
Trust/Jarrolds]

References

Wilson, Hugh and Womersley, Lewis/Ellis, Richard 1982 *Chatham Historic Dockyard Study on Economic and Environmental Opportunities*

Charewud

Barrar hill

west marsh

Saint marshie

Teyarhil

orwd

rmsbery

Stroud

ii west

Chattam

Gillinga

Saint maryes

Lamport

2 'The chief arsenal of the Royal Navy and of Great Britain'[1]

Chatham, the Royal Navy and a wider world

Andrew Lambert

For 400 years Chatham Dockyard occupied a critical place in English/British history, the shipyard, storehouse and depot for much of the Royal Navy in peace and war. As Britain became a global sea-power empire, the dockyard expanded to build and maintain the fleet that made Britain great, assuming global significance.

Chatham's consequence was a product of geography. When the Low Countries and the River Scheldt became part of the Holy Roman and then Spanish empires in the 16th century, the Scheldt switched from a trade artery to the axis for a continental invasion, especially after Henry VIII broke with the Roman Church. His decisions turned the Thames Estuary and the coast of Kent into a strategic front line in the 1540s, against the danger that endured 400 years as a succession of continental powers threatened to invade England or destroy the maritime commerce on which it depended. Only a powerful navy, able to command the narrow seas, could ensure national security. In peacetime such a fleet would be a mighty symbol of strength, one that could be mobilised to deter hostile powers, in a ceremonial display of political resolve.

Originally moored at Woolwich and Deptford on the crowded tidal Thames, the Navy Royal moved to the Medway in 1547, anchored to the north of Rochester Bridge, a sheltered location with ample space 'for the whole Navy Royal to ride in security'.[2] The deep, slow-moving, tortuous river was relatively narrow, easily commanded by shore batteries. When the ships arrived, a storehouse was hired at Gillingham, a shore facility that grew into a massive dockyard. The threat of war with Spain prompted Queen Elizabeth to order the construction of expensive artillery forts at Upnor and Gillingham in 1559. Additional defences against land and, latterly, air threats were added over the centuries, costly testimony to the national consequence of the fleet, its vulnerability while lying in ordinary, without guns, masts or, critically, men, and of the dockyard that sustained it.

The outbreak of war with Spain in 1585 prompted the installation of a chain between Upnor and the opposite bank of the river to stop attacking ships under the guns of the fort.[3] The object was obvious. In 1570 local politician William Lambarde's historical/geographical survey of Kent celebrated the creation of a new national identity around the Tudor dynasty, an English Church and the strength of the Royal Navy, long before the Armada cast a rosy retrospective glow over the Elizabethan project. Printed in 1576, *The Perambulation of Kent* praised Henry VIII for building fortifications at Deal and Sandgate, and Elizabeth for creating the mighty navy that lay at anchor in Gillingham Reach, linking the Tudor fleet to Herodotus's account of the Delphic oracle telling the Athenians to trust their fate to 'the wooden walls'. The power and majesty of the English fleet was a cause for celebration, 'the feare of outward warres removed, … and the river fraught with these strong and serviceable Ships sufficiently'.[4] Historian William Camden developed Lambarde's analysis, describing Chatham as home to

> the best appointed fleet that ever the Sun saw, ready upon all emergent
> occasions, and built at great expence by the most serene Queen Elizabeth
> for the safety of her Kingdoms, and the terror of her enemies; who also
> for the security of it, hath raised a fort [Upnor] upon the bank.[5]

These Tudor texts highlighted the deterrent role of the fleet: they were published to warn potential aggressors. In 1588 Philip II of Spain was well aware of the fleet at Chatham, advising his admiral to pray for victory.

Keeping the fleet ready for war required a growing force of skilled shipwrights and tradesmen, along with storehouses and workshops ashore, exploiting Kent's ample reserves of oak and elm shipbuilding timber, and easy access to Baltic naval stores, ranging from masts and plank to pitch, tar, hemp and flax. Local shipbuilding and iron founding industries enhanced the attraction of a location with excellent road and river communications to London and the other Royal dockyards and arsenals.

In 1570, 60 shipwrights were overhauling two warships, while the development of gated dry docks proved critical to the long-term maintenance of the fleet. By the mid-17th century Chatham had four docks, more than any other English dockyard, or any other navy. Dry docks were major investments, reflecting the Navy's central role in national security, economic activity and diplomatic prestige. Insular England could not risk being caught by surprise before the fleet was ready for sea. Unlike the continental powers, England's security depended on warships; land defences existed to protect them.

The Elizabethan state remained anxious about a surprise attack, constantly amending mobilisation plans, and occasionally putting them into effect as relations with Habsburg Spain deteriorated across the 1570s and 1580s. These plans linked the impressments of seafarers, whose number and distribution were urgently examined, to mobilise the fleet, a costly process that could not be sustained in peacetime. These plans proved effective in 1587, when the fleet was mobilised in three months; the Spanish Armada sailed after three years, without achieving the same level of efficiency.[6] To man the fleet Chatham became the rendezvous for seamen impressed into naval service, and gave its name to the Chatham Chest, a contribution-based charity set up to care for wounded sailors after the Armada Campaign.

Chatham had been chosen because the most likely and the greatest threat came from Spain, which ruled the Low Countries, and could launch an invasion from the River Scheldt. Protestant England, fearing a Catholic Spanish invasion, steadily built up the fleet and occupied the key invasion ports of Vlissingen and Briel in 1585, prompting Spain to declare war. The anchorage at the Nore, close by the confluence of Medway and Thames and the small fort and harbour at Sheerness, provided an operational base that enhanced Chatham's strategic role.

Chatham became a theatre of national power, a place to display the might of the state to visiting heads of state. Not only were the warships at Chatham 'emblems of royal power, emphasised by costly decoration', but foreigners were actively encouraged to visit the fleet, the ultimate symbol of English might. In 1602 the Duke of Stettin was highly impressed; the Danish king Christian IV, who had built his own prestige fleet, arrived in 1606. While the early Stuart kings visited Chatham, and Charles I increased the fleet, Chatham supported Parliament in the Civil War. With power shifting to the City of London, the yard witnessed a dramatic increase in expenditure under the Commonwealth. Yet when unpaid sailors and shipwrights from Chatham marched on London in 1653, they were violently suppressed.[7]

Chatham was ideally placed to take a central role in the three Anglo-Dutch wars between 1652 and 1674, wars punctuated by a succession of major fleet battles, many within a hundred miles of the dockyard, requiring extensive repairs, fresh supplies and ever more manpower. In 1667 a poverty-stricken Stuart monarchy paid off the fleet, assuming the Second Anglo-Dutch War would be resolved by ongoing diplomacy. Instead, the Dutch sought diplomatic advantage in a long-matured attack on Chatham, the ultimate symbol of English power, the basis of their claim to sovereignty at sea, and home to a fleet intimately connected with King Charles II. Having overrun Sheerness, demolished the fort and advanced up the Medway, capturing or burning four great flagships, the

Burning of the English Fleet near Chatham (19–24 June 1667), Willem Schellinks, 1667–78.

[Rijksmuseum Amsterdam]

The Arrival of the *Royal Charles* following her capture during the Dutch Raid, depicted by Jeronumus van Diest (II) in 1667. [Rijskmuseum Amsterdam]

Ships Laid Up in the Medway, Netherlandisch School, c 1675. [National Maritime Museum, Greenwich, London, Caird Collection]

Dutch were stopped by the turn of the tide and the guns at Upnor. While the dockyard survived largely unscathed, the Dutch humiliated the king by turning the captured flagship *Royal Charles* into a tourist attraction. The defences were hastily upgraded and extended up to Sheerness, reflecting Chatham's critical role in national security. Several warships were laid up in other dockyards to reduce the risk of another such raid.[8]

Critically, Chatham was still expanding, building ships to replace those lost in 1667, and servicing the fleet for the inevitable Third Anglo-Dutch War of 1672–4. In May 1688, King James II visited the dockyard and the Thames defences, recognising the danger of a Dutch invasion.[9] This time the Dutch landed an army at Brixham, having sailed past the English fleet, wind-bound in the Thames. By 1689 William of Orange was king, and the Dutch were allies, shifting the focus of naval warfare south and west, and a new fleet base was hastily constructed at Plymouth. Even so, the largest ships were still laid up at Chatham over the winter. When the Nine Years' War ended in 1697, 12 of the 17 three-decked flagships were laid up at Chatham, the other 5 at Portsmouth, while the Medway also housed almost half of the large two-decked battleships.[10]

The annual upkeep of the Royal Navy and the Royal dockyards had dominated English defence spending since the 1540s, binding Crown and Parliament to a shared agenda, although the necessary funding remained a political battleground. The disaster of 1667 followed Parliament's refusal to provide the king with adequate funds. This changed during the post-1688 Revolution Settlement, which created a constitutional monarchy, with the Crown, landed wealth and the commercial sector sharing power. The new system facilitated the creation of a national debt and the Bank of England to mobilise national wealth for war. After

The Royal Prince Before the Wind, Jan Karel Donatus van Beecq. The Royal Navy's first 100-gun ship was launched at Chatham in 1670. [National Maritime Museum, Greenwich, London, Caird Collection]

a French naval victory at Beachy Head in 1690, the country faced an invasion, but large loans were raised to rebuild the fleet. The restored fleet recovered command of the sea at Barfleur/La Hougue in 1692, the first act of a new English state.

By 1707 Great Britain had become a fiscal-military state, using efficient taxation and credit-based financial instruments, including the national debt and the Bank of England, to sustain large-scale naval warfare for prolonged periods. Costly naval dockyards, the most potent symbols of the new state 'were, by the standards of the day, immense enterprises. They were the largest industrial units in the country' and 'operated on a scale quite unlike that of civilian industry and commerce'.[11] Chatham, the largest dockyard, was the ultimate symbol of national might, a place the king would visit to demonstrate his role as national figurehead.

Daniel Defoe understood that synergy of money, power and prestige: his *Tour through the Whole Island of Britain* of the mid-1720s highlighted Chatham's unparalleled scale, the impressive number of ships in ordinary, and the efficient system of placing the guns, gear, small arms and other stores of each ship in a separate storehouse, ensuring rapid mobilisation. Other storehouses were packed with timber, rope and iron to build new ships. He used Chatham to highlight the uniquely naval nature of British power only 30 years after the 'Glorious Revolution', linking the nation's wealth and stability to the naval power that secured an expanding overseas trade.

Chatham, the essential connection between economic expansion and domestic prosperity, 'the chief arsenal of the Royal Navy and of Great Britain', was the largest in the world, 'monstrously great and extensive'. The risks of war had been addressed since the humiliation of 1667.

> This alarm gave England such a sense of the consequence of the river Medway, and of the docks and yards at Chatham, and of the danger the Royal Navy lay exposed to there, that all these doors which were open then, are lock'd up and sufficiently barr'd since that time; and 'tis not now in the power of any nation under heaven, no, tho' they should be masters-at-sea, unless they were masters at land too at the same time, to give us such another affront; for besides all the castles, lines of guns, and platforms on each side of the river Medway, as we go up, … there is now a royal fort built at the point on the Isle of Shepey, call'd Sheerness, which guards that entrance into the river: this is a regular and so complete a fortification, and has such a line of heavy cannon commanding the mouth of the river, that no man of war, or fleet of men of war, would attempt to pass it as the Dutch did, or at least could not effect without hazard of being torn to pieces by those batteries.[12]

Yet the massive investment in naval infrastructure at Chatham between 1688 and the 1720s created a problem. For much of the 18th century it was in the wrong place; increasingly, global wars with France had focused naval activity on the Western Approaches. Portsmouth and Plymouth maintained the great fleets in wartime, leaving Chatham to mobilise the reserve, and build and carry out major reconstructions. Chatham lent shipwrights to other, busier, yards in the 1740s.[13]

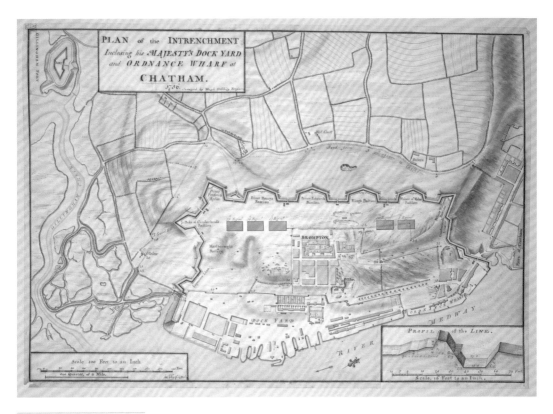

A Plan of the Intrenchement of Chatham. Shows the first defensive line of fortifications built to defend the dockyard and the Ordnance Wharf at Chatham in 1756. [© The British Library Board (Maps K.Top.16 (40))]

The problem of strategic geography was compounded by a shoaling river that rendered the dockyard increasingly difficult to access from the sea. In 1744 a sudden squall capsized the 60-gun ship *Pembroke* in the river, with heavy loss of life. With Britannia dominant at sea, the old emphasis on security had been replaced by the need to get the fleet to sea quickly. More ships were laid up on the south coast, better located for a war with France. Sheerness became an operational base with a small dockyard, reducing the need to navigate the Medway. Yet rather than abandon Chatham, the Earl of Sandwich, First Lord of the Admiralty in 1773, observed:

> if it is kept singly to its proper use as a building yard possibly more useful service may be obtained from it than any other dockyard … the great extent of the yard which faces the river and the great length of the harbour which has room to moor half the fleet of England of a moderate draught of water, … the best use to be made of this port now, is to build or repair ships sent from Portsmouth or Plymouth, therefore all improvements at this yard should be for that end, in preference to any other consideration. Only smaller ships should be laid up constantly here.[14]

Sandwich's mania for order and neatness changed the appearance of the yard,[15] turning the largest industrial unit in Western Europe into a fit place for a royal visit. King George III's inspection in 1774 reinforced Sandwich's message, one of many events he organised to reconnect

nation, monarchy and navy into an idealised vision of power, prosperity and peace. The dockyards were used to promote a navalist national agenda. Chatham also attracted the attention of foreign spies, although any useful intelligence they gathered was countered by the overwhelming impression of power, which offered the best hope of deterring French aggression.

To increase the effective lives of the great warships, the number of slipways and dry docks at Chatham was increased, so they could be built slowly, their timbers seasoned at every stage of construction. Chatham's most famous product, HMS *Victory*, spent six years under construction in No. 2 Dock. This approach emphasised the fleet's deterrent role, and the need to reduce the consumption of scarce timber remained central to peacetime shipbuilding to the end of the era of wooden walls.

The London-based Navy Board, which administered the dockyards, commissioned a superb image of the yard from topographical artist Joseph Farrington, allowing the Board to visualise the work at Chatham.[16] The picture included part of the reserve fleet: when the 12-year-old Horatio Nelson joined the Navy at Chatham, *Victory* was among the ships laid up on the river, a silent, static colossus of immense latent power, combining national symbolism, a name with countless battle honours, and the threat of 100 cannon.

In 1755 Chatham acquired an 1,800-man division of Royal Marines, providing the sea-soldiers that formed part of the ship's company. To protect the massive investment in ships and facilities, Chatham's land defences were constantly extended. In 1708–9, high ground to the east of the yard was purchased, but the 'Chatham Lines' were only begun in the mid-1750s, to meet rumours of a French invasion. Over time, additional works, including Fort Amherst, were added, along with growing barrack accommodation for the necessary troops. These included the Royal Engineers, the scientific corps dedicated to building and capturing fortresses. In 1812 a new school for Royal Engineer personnel at Chatham turned British strategy into operational procedure.[17] This became clear when British forces captured and destroyed Sevastopol dockyard in

1855.[18] The large local garrison and powerful defences created across the centuries only emphasised Chatham's critical place in national defence.

During the wars of the French Revolution and Empire (1793–1815), Chatham was once again on the front line, supporting the great fleets that blockaded the Scheldt and the Dutch coast, where Napoleon assembled a battlefleet at Antwerp. Those fleets ensured the emperor's ships never left the Scheldt. Chatham also supported the great fleets dispatched to the Baltic in 1801, and between 1807 and 1813 fleets largely composed of older, smaller ships that needed extensive maintenance.

Wartime Chatham also focused on major repair work, with Sir Robert Seppings, master shipwright at Chatham, re-engineering the wooden warship to reflect the dynamic tactics of Nelson's era and the shortage of seasoned timber. Seppings' triangulated frame increased structural rigidity, used smaller timbers, and integrated the hitherto open bow and stern structures into the frame, enabling wooden warships to become bigger, more durable, and capable of using steam engines. Seppings' ideas were adopted by the Admiralty, while he became both a surveyor of the Navy and a fellow of the Royal Society.[19] Chatham remained central to naval innovation.

The growing problem of navigating the Medway prompted the idea of replacing all the dockyards on the Thames and Medway with a new facility at Northfleet. The cost of the plan and the development of steam-powered bucket dredgers saved Chatham. By the time Napoleon was finally defeated, much of the dockyard infrastructure was worn out and

The Battle of Trafalgar, 21 October 1805, J M W Turner. Nelson's Chatham-built flagship Victory underwent a great repair at Chatham in the years immediately before the battle.
[National Maritime Museum, Greenwich, London, Greenwich Hospital Collection]

outdated by new technologies, including steam power for emptying the dry docks and powering sawmills. The Navy decided to build all future capital ships and frigates in the Royal dockyards, in the interests of quality control, a decision that required additional covered slipways. The frigate HMS *Unicorn* at Dundee, the last surviving warship built in the 1820s, represents the era; the ship was placed in reserve upon completion, and never commissioned. Superior construction methods, including the Seppings frame, have kept her afloat ever since. At the same time, Sheerness, the operational base that linked Chatham with the fleet, was completely rebuilt to ensure the fleet at Chatham could be mobilised and sent to sea in an emergency.[20] This costly programme reflected the anxiety of post-1815 governments to avoid another costly conflict. The fleet laid up in the Medway after 1815, approximately one-third of the Navy, was intended for Baltic and North Sea operations. The Low Countries remained the focal point of British strategy for the next 150 years, while the Russian Baltic Fleet was growing.

Yet the Napoleonic era had finally shifted the Navy's focal point from the Medway to Portsmouth, which acquired additional prestige, hosting a Royal Fleet review in April 1814 attended by the Prince Regent, the Tsar and the King of Prussia. Spithead became the theatre of national glory, where naval might, royal prestige and deterrence were signalled. The Nore, tarnished by memories of the 1797 mutiny, poor road communications and a challenging micro-climate, simply could not compete. When Victoria and Albert decided to build a family retreat at Osborne on the Isle of Wight, the process was complete. Every journey to Osborne turned into a royal visit to Portsmouth, including Chatham's greatest ship HMS *Victory*, permanently moored off the Hampshire dockyard. Lacking a parade ground, or even a coast, Chatham was less frequented by the elite, British and foreign.

After 1815 most warships made their final departure from Britain at Portsmouth or Plymouth, even if they were built and manned at Chatham, heading out into a wider world beyond Europe. Although Chatham slipped into the background, relative anonymity masked continuing consequence. Chatham played a major role in the Crimean War (1854–6), supporting the British Baltic fleet that threatened Russia's capital city, St Petersburg. Chatham supplied the steam-powered fleet with food, fuel, ammunition and regular drafts of men. Each winter it began a four-month cycle of refits and repairs, to prepare for another campaign. New vessels built in private shipyards were fitted out at Chatham, while the armoured battery *Aetna*, completed in 1856, was the first armoured warship to be built by a Royal dockyard.[21]

Chatham endured and expanded. In 1821 civil engineer John Rennie proposed a major redevelopment, which involved diverting the Medway to create a massive floating basin and new slipways, emphasising the construction, repair and preservation of the fleet. The basin would store the entire battlefleet. Rennie's project was too radical for an economically challenged era without obvious naval rivals. Expansion plans revived in the late 1840s to address a resurgent French fleet and the menace of a steam-powered re-run of 1667. This made the original advantage of a relatively secure location down a narrow winding river attractive, especially when ironclad warships replaced wooden walls. With coastal

The Fighting Temeraire. J M W
Turner's depiction of the Chatham-
built second rate being towed to
the breakers yard by steam tug in
1838. *Temeraire* was second in line
to *Victory* at Trafalgar.
[National Gallery]

dockyards exposed to bombardment and attack, Chatham would be
more secure than Portsmouth or Plymouth, especially with new forts
commanding the river. Consequently, when the dramatic expansion
of the French fleet and dockyards in the 1850s made it imperative to
increase British dockyard capacity to sustain the fleet in a war, Chatham
was selected. In 1858 the Admiralty proposed extending Chatham to
replace the building capacity lost when the cramped yards at Woolwich
and Deptford closed.[22] In 1860, new forts at Sheerness, on the Isle of
Grain and inside the Medway at Hoo and Darnet updated Chatham's
fixed defences for the ironclad era, keeping hostile ships beyond gun
range. Within a few years major dredging operations improved access to
the yard, enabling it to continue building and servicing capital ships. By
the time this work was complete, the mid-century Anglo-French race in
dockyard infrastructure had ended.[23]

The dockyard extension, which involved 1,000 convict labourers,
embanked St Mary's Island and created more floating basin
accommodation than the rest of the Royal dockyards combined. The
extension increased the size of the yard from 97 to 380 acres, including
four new dry docks to support the latest warships. Largely complete
by 1870, the project ensured Chatham remained fully engaged as
shipbuilding shifted to steam and iron, beginning with the Navy's first
iron-hulled armoured warship, HMS *Achilles*, emphasising the yard's
continuing role as a centre of shipbuilding expertise. Chatham's proximity

to London, then the world centre of iron shipbuilding, was a factor in the
decision.[24] Dockyard construction enabled the Admiralty to check the
cost and quality of private shipbuilding and ensure the dockyards had the
necessary skills to repair damaged ships in wartime.

Once the extension was complete, the convict prisons were replaced
by naval barracks, housing sailors and officers between commissions, a
vital asset for any naval base after continuous-service commission-only
engagements in the mid-1850s. The new dockyard, barracks and Royal
Marine facilities, completed in the 1880s, restored Chatham's status as
one of the three big dockyards, home to roughly one-third of the service,
the mobilisation point for Eastern England, and the strategic hub for any
war in the eastern Channel, the North Sea and the Baltic.

Shipbuilding remained in the Old Yard, initially in No. 2 Dock,
and then on No. 7 Slip, which was converted to accommodate larger
iron and steel ships down to the armoured cruiser HMS *Shannon* of
1906. Chatham's last battleship HMS *Africa* was launched from 8 Slip
immediately to the north in 1905. Thereafter, cruisers and, increasingly,
submarines were the main output of the yard; the latter became a
specialisation. The last ship to be built at Chatham was the Canadian
submarine HMCS *Okanagan*, launched in 1966, ending 400 years of
warship building on the site. Submarine-building expertise brought
the Royal Navy's first nuclear submarine refuelling facility to Chatham,
adding another toxic legacy to the industrial waste of ages past.

Across the 20th century, defence spending steadily became less
dominant in the national economy, while security fell behind domestic
economic concerns in the political process. In an age of distant imperial
wars, efficient dockyards and silent, stationary reserve fleets no longer
seemed to be the obvious symbols of national power. As the fiscal-military
state began the journey to welfare state, old certainties would be lost.
Even in the two world wars Chatham was rarely in the spotlight, even if

The launch of Chatham's last battleship, HMS *Africa*, in 1905 from No. 8 Slip – immediately to the north of the historic dockyard.
[Chatham Historic Dockyard Trust]

King George V's 1917 visit to Chatham – the Women's Royal Naval Service had only just been formed.
[Chatham Historic Dockyard Trust]

Kenneth Shoesmith's evocative
poster for a mid-1930s Navy Week
at Chatham and Sheerness.
[Chatham Historic Dockyard Trust]

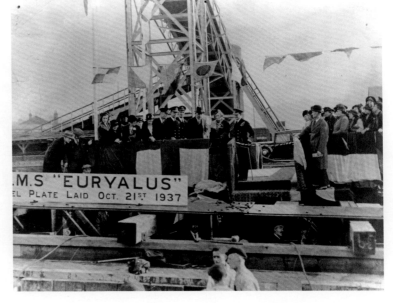

Laying the Keel ceremony for
the cruiser HMS *Euryalus* in
1937. Launched in June 1939,
she was commissioned in 1941
and saw extensive service in the
Mediterranean and British
Pacific Fleets.
[Chatham Historic Dockyard Trust]

Launch of **HMCS** *Okanagan* at Chatham in 1966. *Okanagan* was the last warship built at Chatham. [Chatham Historic Dockyard Trust]

it was on the front line, exposed to aerial attack, and critically engaged in sustaining the naval war. Although the dockyard made a massive contribution to the war effort, it was already on borrowed time. As the British Empire and the global naval force that had secured it shrank, hard choices had to be made. Closure was seriously considered in the late 1940s: Portsmouth and Plymouth were the core naval assets.[25] The final chapter opened in 1958, when the historic Nore Command was abolished, Sheerness dockyard closed, and several facilities at Chatham wound up. Yet when the end came, it did so with brutal speed.

In August 1980, the government publicly committed itself to keeping all four dockyards. In 1981 the Nott Review reversed that decision: Chatham would close in 1984, just after the Falklands conflict had re-emphasised the critical role of dockyard expertise in national security.[26]

Chatham Dockyard sat at the heart of a dynamic complex, one that combined the construction and repair of the Royal Navy, the nation's primary instrument of power on the world stage, with local defences, troops, and supporting industries from forestry and food production to iron founding and brick-making, a business prompted by local clay and constant naval demand. It embodied the fiscal military state that made Britain a great power. For 400 years Chatham, at one time the largest industrial facility in the world, was a showcase for the symbols of national power: visitors arriving by road and river were impressed by great ships, massive buildings and ceaseless activity. The dockyard acquired classically proportioned buildings of power, architectural and

The Victorian Dockyard extension
– an aerial view taken in the
late 1970s/early 1980s showing
the three 1880s basins and the
Edwardian Naval Barracks HMS
Pembroke top right. HMS *Endurance*,
the Royal Navy's Antarctic Patrol
ship was Chatham based and seen
here in dry dock in her distinctive
red hull and white superstructure.
[Chatham Historic Dockyard Trust]

A nuclear submarine leaves the
Bullnose locks after refuelling
and refit.
[Chatham Historic Dockyard Trust]

cultural references reinforcing the sea-power message, providing kings
and princes with suitable spaces in which to digest their dinner, and their
experience. Spies came to fathom the secrets of British success, and walls
went up to restrict their view, as they had in Venice a few centuries before.

Another frequent visitor, the artist J M W Turner, turned ships and forts, the Medway and the dockyard into panoramas that reflected and reinforced ideas of Britain's greatness just as the age of sail elided into that of steam.[27] Turner's Chatham was a quiet place, packed with latent power and signs of progress, a central plank in the unique, specific national identity of a fiscal-military sea-power state. The dockyard still conveys the might and majesty of an earlier age when Britannia ruled the waves, and Chatham sharpened her trident.

Notes

1   Defoe, Daniel 1991 *A Tour through the Whole Island of Britain*, eds Furbank, P N and Owens, W R. London: Yale University Press, 46.
2   Rodger, Nicholas A M 1997 *The Safeguard of the Sea: A Naval History of Britain: Volume 1: 660–1649*. London: Harper Collins, 336. The anchorage was mapped as early as 1562. BL Cottonian.
3   Saunders, Andrew D 2008 *Upnor Castle*. London: English Heritage, 5–10.
4   Lambarde, William 1576 *Perambulation of Kent: Containing the Description, Hystorie and Customs of that Shyre*. London, 129, 155, 311–15, 328. The 1826 edition included Lambarde's manuscript amendments.
5   Camden, William 1695 *Britannia*. London, 194.
6   Rodger, Nicholas A M 1997 *The Safeguard of the Sea: A Naval History of Britain, Vol 1: 660–1649*, 327–79.
7   Rodger, Nicholas A M 2004 *Command of the Ocean: A Naval History of Britain, Vol II: 1649–1815*. London: Allen Lane, 19.
8   Saunders, 14–15.
9   Ehrman, John 1953 *The Navy in the War of William III*. Cambridge: Cambridge University Press, 212, 214–18.
10 Ehrman, 452, 621.
11 The key text on this process is Brewer, John 1989 *The Sinews of Power: War, Money and the English State 1688–1783*. London: Unwin Hyman. See 35–6.
12 Defoe, 47–8.
13 Baugh, Daniel 1965 *British Naval Administration in the Age of Walpole*. Princeton, NJ: Princeton University Press, 265–70.
14 Dunster, Sandra 2013 *The Medway Towns: River, Docks and Urban Life*. London: Phillimore, 69.
15 Rodger, Nicholas A M 1993 *The Insatiable Earl: A Life of John Mountagu, 4th Earl of Sandwich*. London: Harper Collins, 144.
16 National Maritime Museum. The picture took nine years to complete.
17 Kendall, Peter 2013 *The Royal Engineers at Chatham 1750–2012*. Swindon: English Heritage, 67–70.
18 Lambert, Andrew 2011 *The Crimean War, British Grand Strategy against Russia, 1853–1856*. Aldershot: Ashgate.
19 Lambert, Andrew 1991 *The Last Sailing Battlefleet: Maintaining Naval Mastery 1815–1850*. London: Conway.
20 Lord Melville (First Lord of the Admiralty) to Lord Liverpool (Prime Minister) 28 July 1818: BL Add. MSS 38272 ff.334-42 Liverpool Papers.
21 Winfield, Rif 2014 *British Warships in the Age of Sail 1817–1863: Design, Construction, Careers and Fates*. Seaforth Publishing, 196.
22 Walker Memo 20 May 1858: ADM 1/5698 pt. 1.
23 Hamilton, Ian 1993 *Anglo-French Naval Rivalry 1840–1870*. Oxford: Oxford University Press, 202–4.
24 Evans, David 2004 *Building the Steam Navy: Dockyards, Technology and the Creation of the Victorian Battle Fleet, 1830–1906*. London: English Heritage, 155, 163–5, 181–2. Quotation from William Scamp CHD Doc. 10.

25   Admiralty Board Memo 1993 'The Revised Restricted Fleet, 1949'. *British Naval Documents 1294–1960*. London Navy Records Society, 805.
26   Grove, Eric J 1987 *Vanguard to Trident: British Naval Policy since World War II*. London: Bodley Head, 213, 221–9, 351–3.
27   Shanes, Eric 2016 *J M W Turner – A Life in Art. Young Mr Turner. The First Forty Years, 1775–1815*. New Haven, CT and London: Yale University Press, 277–9, 293.

References

Admiralty Board Memo 1993 'The Revised Restricted Fleet, 1949'. *British Naval Documents 1294–1960*. London Navy Records Society

Baugh, Daniel 1965 *British Naval Administration in the Age of Walpole*. Princeton, NJ: Princeton University Press

Brewer, John 1989 *The Sinews of Power: War, Money and the English State 1688–1783*. London: Unwin Hyman

Camden, William 1695 *Britannia*. London

Defoe, Daniel 1991 *A Tour through the Whole Island of Britain*, eds Furbank, P N and Owens, W R. London: Yale University Press

Dunster, Sandra 2013 *The Medway Towns: River, Docks and Urban Life*. London: Phillimore

Ehrman, John 1953 *The Navy in the War of William III*. Cambridge: Cambridge University Press

Evans, David 2004 *Building the Steam Navy: Dockyards, Technology and the Creation of the Victorian Battle Fleet, 1830–1906*. London: English Heritage

Grove, Eric J 1987 *Vanguard to Trident: British Naval Policy since World War II*. London: Bodley Head

Hamilton, Ian 1993 *Anglo-French Naval Rivalry 1840–1870*. Oxford: Oxford University Press

Kendall, Peter 2013 *The Royal Engineers at Chatham 1750–2012*. Swindon: English Heritage

Lambarde, William 1576 *Perambulation of Kent: Containing the Description, Hystorie and Customs of that Shyre*. London

Lambert, Andrew 1991 *The Last Sailing Battlefleet: Maintaining Naval Mastery 1815–1850*. London: Conway

Lambert, Andrew 2011 *The Crimean War, British Grand Strategy against Russia, 1853–1856*. Aldershot: Ashgate

Lord Melville (First Lord of the Admiralty) to Lord Liverpool (Prime Minister) 28 July 1818: BL Add. MSS 38272 ff.334-42 Liverpool Papers

Rodger, Nicholas A M 1993 *The Insatiable Earl: A Life of John Mountagu, 4th Earl of Sandwich*. London: Harper Collins

Rodger, Nicholas A M 1997 *The Safeguard of the Sea: A Naval History of Britain: Volume 1: 660–1649*. London: Harper Collins

Rodger, Nicholas A M 2004 *Command of the Ocean: A Naval History of Britain, Vol II: 1649–1815*. London: Allen Lane

Saunders, Andrew D 2008 *Upnor Castle*. London: English Heritage

Shanes, Eric 2016 *J M W Turner – A Life in Art. Young Mr Turner. The First Forty Years, 1775–1815*. New Haven, CT and London: Yale University Press

Walker Memo 20 May 1858: ADM 1/5698 pt. 1

Winfield, Rif 2014 *British Warships in the Age of Sail 1817–1863: Design, Construction, Careers and Fates*. Seaforth Publishing

3 'The most complete dockyard of the Age of Sail'

Jonathan Coad

This arresting claim was crucial in helping secure a future for the historic heart of Chatham Dockyard following the 1981 government announcement that the naval base was to close in 1984. Is the claim justified, and what makes Chatham Historic Dockyard uniquely important? The answer lies in a combination of the unpredictable chances of history, the mixed fortunes of the dockyard, foresight, appreciation and, in the end, a lot of hard work and goodwill.

The Royal Navy was first established as a permanent organisation by Henry VII at the end of the 15th century. Constructing, maintaining and repairing the king's ships demanded extensive, well-equipped and permanent shore facilities. These had to be adjacent to sheltered water to allow warships to anchor securely to be laid up or over-wintered at a time when naval operations were almost invariably confined to the summer months. Portsmouth harbour, with its relatively safe anchorages, became the location around 1492 for the Navy's first shore base. At its centre was a primitive dry dock, for long the most costly feature of a naval base and one that soon gave its name to the whole establishment – literally, the yard round the dry dock, although not all dockyards, including Chatham, had such a facility from the beginning. Portsmouth was followed by dockyards at Woolwich and Deptford in the second decade of the 16th century. These could take advantage of the ship-building skills along the Thames and were also conveniently close to Henry VIII's palace at Greenwich. By the 1540s, the growth in the size of the fleet and the pressure on moorings adjacent to the two Thames yards was leading to increasing use of the River Medway just below Rochester Bridge as a safe and secure anchorage for laying up warships. Chatham Dockyard, which shifted slightly down river to its present location in 1618, can trace its beginnings to 1547 when a storehouse was hired at Gillingham.

In the 17th century, when the Dutch were England's principal maritime rival and enemy, Chatham's strategic location with its proximity to the North Sea saw it develop into England's most important naval base, supplemented from the middle of the century by a small yard at Harwich, construction of Sheerness Dockyard at the mouth of the Medway, and the creation of a minor supply base at Deal. At Chatham itself, the number of buildings and facilities built towards the end of the century reflected its primacy and role as a fleet base where substantial numbers of warships could be kept awaiting fitting out when required, with the dockyard, ordnance yard and victualling facilities essential for this work. This strategic importance was not to last. By the early 18th century, rivalry with Spain and France and Britain's expanding worldwide trade saw naval focus shift westwards towards the Atlantic and beyond. This was

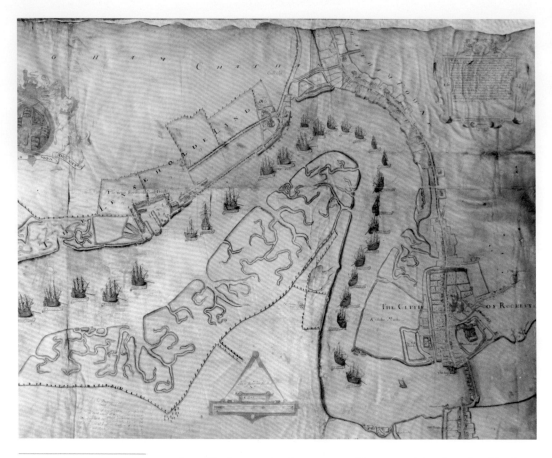

Chatham Dockyard c 1633, showing the storehouse, workshops and houses grouped round the working area surrounding the double and single dock. To the right is the Ropery. This is one of the earliest illustrations of any dockyard and is part of a painting at Alnwick Castle. [Duke of Northumberland, Alnwick Castle]

reflected in the growing importance of Portsmouth Dockyard and in the 1690s by the construction of Plymouth (now Devonport) Dockyard along with a cruiser and supply base at Kinsale in southern Ireland. The two south-coast dockyards were increasingly seen as the principal fleet bases, and Chatham was never to regain its pre-eminence.

Chatham's changing status nevertheless took some time to become apparent. In 1703, when Captain George St Lo, commissioner of the new Plymouth Dockyard, was offered the commissioner's role at Chatham, it was seen as a considerable promotion, although he considered the official residence at the Medway to be markedly inferior to that at Plymouth. St Lo solved the problem by successfully petitioning for a new and larger house to be built at Chatham, where it still stands, the oldest intact dockyard building remaining in any of the naval bases. At the then northern end of the dockyard, the surviving mast pond is contemporary, an early plan describing it as 'new' in 1704. Both were constructed at the start of a period that was to see a sustained and astonishing rise in the size of the British fleet, which in 1695 numbered some 112 line-of-battleships and around 46 cruisers. Sixty years later, totals had more than doubled, and as warships were being built to larger dimensions, the combined tonnage had tripled. This expansion kept all the dockyards busy with construction and maintenance and ensured that by the middle of the 18th

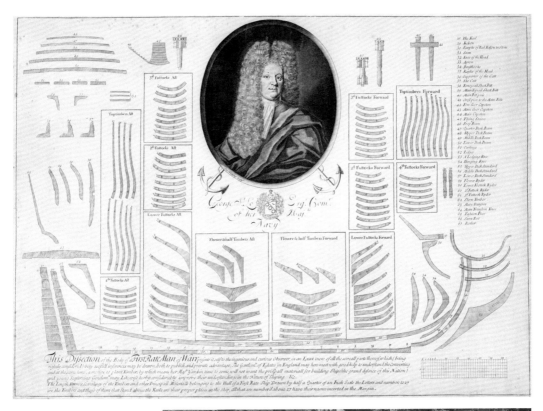

Captain George St Lo, with the
timbers of a first-rate ship of
the line.
[National Maritime Museum]

Medway House, built as a house for
the dockyard commissioner in 1704
and the oldest intact dockyard
building in the country.
[Geoff Watkins Aerial Imaging
South East]

century the Royal Navy and its extensive shore facilities had, de facto,
arguably become the largest industrial organisation in the world. For the
British fleet, the 18th and first half of the 19th centuries were the great
'Age of Sail'.

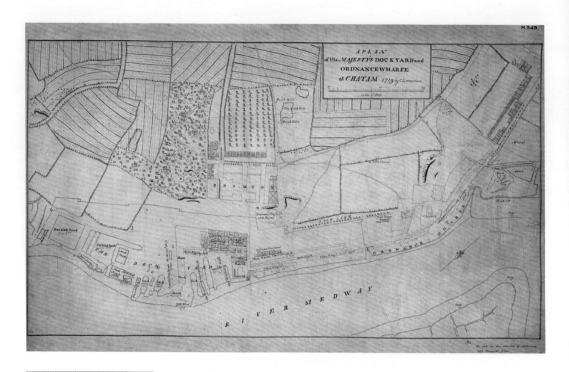

M 345

Chatham Dockyard in 1719 showing the dockyard's growth along the Medway since 1633. This plan by Lemprière shows the newly acquired land to its rear and the position of the existing Main Gate. After this expansion there were to be few boundary changes for almost a century.
[The National Archives]

At Chatham, further land for expansion of the dockyard was acquired along its eastern boundary and in 1716 enclosed by the existing dockyard wall with its imposing Main Gate and little 'watch towers'. Much of this land was occupied by a new terrace for the senior dockyard officers, with its spacious walled gardens built between 1722 and 1731, allowing the older housing and buildings in the centre of the yard to be demolished. Part of the space gained was occupied by the existing 1723 Clocktower Building, the oldest surviving naval storehouse. Unusually, this originally incorporated saw pits at one end. South of the Officers' Terrace the contemporary Sail Loft stems from an Admiralty decision in 1716 that the dockyards should manufacture sails rather than depend on unreliable contractors. With the exception of the more utilitarian storehouse, which originally had timber-framed and weather-boarded upper storeys, the rest were solid brick buildings distinguished by their handsome elevations, Vanbrugian crenellated parapets and spacious interiors. This group was the last to be constructed before the Admiralty tacitly had to admit that Chatham could no longer realistically be considered as a fleet base.

This diminution of Chatham's importance was not just a result of the westward shift of Great Britain's maritime focus and changing strategic requirements. A more fundamental problem lay in the shoaling of the River Medway and the problems it was causing for large warships. One of the reasons for founding Sheerness in the mid-1660s had been to enable such ships to have minor repairs and hulls cleaned there, saving an arduous and time-consuming up-river journey. As warships grew larger, this problem worsened. Attempts to dredge the Medway and provide warping posts and buoys for warships to work their way up-river were largely unsuccessful, and by the mid-18th century large warships could

The Main Gate in the later 19th century. This most imposing of dockyard entrances was intended to emphasise the might of the Royal Navy.
[Royal Engineers Museum, Library and Archives]

Part of the 1774 dockyard model showing the Clocktower Building of 1723 in the centre. This is the oldest naval storehouse showing the sawpits at one end and the weather-boarded upper floors replaced in brick in 1802. To the rear is part of the Officers' Terrace. Note the timber stacked in all available spaces.
[Jonathan Coad]

only attempt the journey with favourable winds during spring tides. A list of eight warships ordered from Sheerness to Chatham in 1770 showed that the average time taken then was six weeks, with one ship taking four months and three days, with time mostly spent waiting at Sheerness. These problems, eventually solved by steam dredging in the 19th century, had effectively ended Chatham's role as a fleet base where ease and speeds of access and egress were crucial. Similar shoaling problems and lack of space were also affecting the Thames yards at Deptford and Woolwich, while the infestation of Teredo worms at Sheerness was becoming a problem that limited that cramped yard's utility. One possible solution, briefly considered by the Admiralty in the 1760s, was to close all Thames and Medway yards and establish a new one on the Isle of Grain. Although nothing came of this, largely because of the likely costs, it added to doubts about Chatham's long-term future.

At the same time as a Grain yard was being considered, one of the most ambitious and expensive dockyard modernisation programmes yet undertaken by the Admiralty and Navy Board was well under way to expand, rebuild and modernise the main fleet bases at Portsmouth and Plymouth. Following carefully considered master plans and starting in 1760, works at these yards were spread over more than 40 years. Existing buildings were largely swept away and replaced by well-designed spacious storehouses, workshops, roperies, building slips and additional dry docks. These were carefully arranged in formal layouts and sited to allow more efficient working. A conscious effort was also made to replace wooden buildings by more durable ones constructed of brick or stone, which also helped minimise the risk of fires spreading. When the works were completed, the scale of these two dockyards was unrivalled in Europe.

With growing uncertainty about Chatham's future, very few buildings were constructed in the yard from the mid-1730s to the 1770s and most of these were built of cheaper timber rather than brick. The former was readily available from warships being broken up. One exception was the Joiners' and House Carpenters' Shop, originally planned to be timber-framed, but constructed in 1742 using bricks, probably in deference to its location adjacent to the north end of the Officers' Terrace. The skills of the yard joiners and house carpenters are well shown in the ambitious 1753 timber-framed Mast Houses and Mould Loft, the latter a unique survivor of this type and almost certainly used six years later to draw out the lines of HMS *Victory*. For the great majority of Chatham Dockyard buildings, docks and slips, the middle years of the 18th century remained a period of 'make do', with a shortage of funds even for the most essential maintenance.

The yard's fortunes were to change for the better following the Board of Admiralty's tour of the dockyards in 1773. The Earl of Sandwich, First Lord and one of the most able holders of that office in the 18th century, reported after the Board's visit to Chatham that the access problems of the Medway ruled out the yard's use as a fleet base. Instead he advocated a different future:

> I am now more and more convinced that if it is kept singly to its proper use as a Building Yard, possibly more useful service may be obtained from it than from any other Dockyard in His Majesty's dominions; the great extent of the yard which faces the River, and the great length of the harbour which has room to moor half the fleet of England of a moderate draught of water, are conveniences that are not to be found elsewhere; and it will appear by the repairs that have been carried on during the Visitations [of all the dockyards] I have lately made, that more business in the way of building and repair has been done here than in any one, possibly than in

any two of the other Yards … The best use to be made of this port now is to build and repair ships sent from Portsmouth and Plymouth, therefore all improvements at this yard should be for that end.[1]

Sandwich's 1773 recommendations for Chatham gave the yard a more certain and secure future and justified fresh investment. This was clearly necessary, as Sandwich reported after his 1775 inspection that 'I am sorry to bear testimony that almost all the buildings in Chatham Yard are so ruinous that be the expense what it will, they must be rebuilt before many more years are passed'.[2] In practice this meant only replacing buildings that were beyond sensible repair rather than undertaking a wholesale replanning and rebuilding, with the fortuitous outcome that Chatham has a much higher proportion of its earlier buildings than any other dockyard and is unique in having examples from every decade between 1700 and 1860. Its feel is of a river yard that has gradually evolved along its narrow strip of land beside the Medway.

The buildings erected following Sandwich's recommendations were not all large and architecturally notable. Sandwich had been determined to improve the durability of the British fleet by using only seasoned timber for warship construction or repair. In 1771 the Navy Board had put forward proposals for sufficient timber seasoning sheds for every dockyard to hold a three-year stock of sawn timber. Sandwich championed these proposals and today Chatham has the only two survivors, built c 1775, of these humble but vital ranges of timber-framed and racked sheds with gabled, tiled roofs that were once common in all the dockyards.

A View of Chatham Dockyard, 1774,
by Elias Martin RA.
[Chatham Historic Dockyard Trust]

Part of the 1774 dockyard model. In the foreground is the surviving Mast Houses and Mould Loft and beyond them the two mast ponds. The frames in the latter kept mast timbers submerged.
[Jonathan Coad]

The more obvious and visible monument to Sandwich's drive to revitalise the yard is its narrow southern end, which had to be largely rebuilt and where the major modernisation work was first concentrated. The huge 700ft-long Anchor Wharf storehouse, probably completed in 1785, and the adjacent and slightly younger Fitted Rigging and Storehouse finished some 20 years later dominate the waterfront here and are among the largest of their type, reflecting the need to make maximum use of available space. Behind them stretches the 1,140ft Ropery of 1786–92, replacing the previous all-timber one which had been a serious fire hazard. All the major buildings here largely retain their original interiors, while the Ropery is unique and of outstanding importance in

The southernmost of two timber seasoning sheds at Chatham. These are the last survivors of a sustained campaign in all the dockyards in the 1770s to construct sufficient numbers of these buildings to accommodate a three years' stock of seasoning timber.
[Chatham Historic Dockyard Trust]

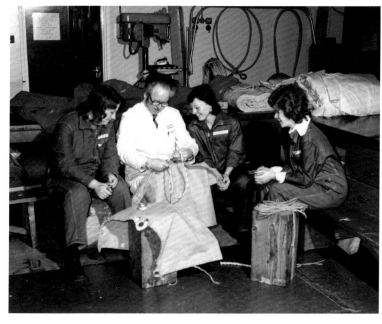

Canvas being worked in the sail loft in 1981. Note the sailmaker's bench.
[Chatham Historic Dockyard Trust]

still producing cordage on machinery, some of which was installed during the Napoleonic Wars.

Modernisation of the southern end of the yard was largely complete by 1805, by which time the country was again at war with Napoleonic France and all the naval bases were fully stretched. By then, too, the Industrial Revolution was starting to have an impact on the dockyards. In 1795 concern that the latter were not benefiting from the growing industrialisation of Britain led the Admiralty to appoint Samuel Bentham to the new post of Inspector General of Naval Works, with a small staff charged with modernising and mechanising the dockyards and liaising with the country's growing number of industrialists, engineers and

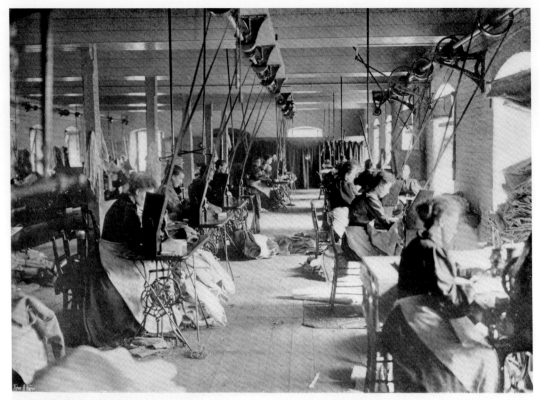

MAKING FLAGS IN THE CHATHAM LOFT.

Wind and weather cause a constant demand for flags of all kinds.
From Photos. specially taken for " Navy & Army Illustrated.'

Part of the sail loft was used for flag making from an early date. This late 19th-century photograph shows flag makers in part of the building.

[Jonathon Coad collection]

contractors. Bentham's small staff also included a civilian architect, the Navy's first such permanent post. Hitherto, responsibility for the layout of dockyards and design of their buildings and engineering works had been the responsibility of the surveyor of the Navy, who generally relied for advice and help from the senior dockyard officers. In 1805, when attention at Chatham was turning to further projects in the central part of the dockyard, Edward Holl was the architect, a post he held until his death in 1823. Holl was prolific, designing handsome, well-proportioned buildings reflecting contemporary late-Georgian Regency style. He was also probably the most experienced architect in the country in the use of cast and wrought iron for structural and fire-proofing purposes, and a number of his buildings remain in the home yards and overseas, notably at Port Royal and Bermuda. At Chatham, a small and varied group reflects his versatility and talents and tie the yard firmly into the wider Industrial Revolution then under way in Britain.

Holl's first building here was the dockyard chapel, authorised in 1804 and completed in 1810, superseding a series of hulks that had served as floating chapels secured alongside the river wall. Unusually, rather than using contractors, much of the construction apparently was done by dockyard employees. Inside is the original tiered gallery with its box pews.

The thin, fluted cast iron columns supporting the galleries are possibly the first such use of this material for structural purposes in the dockyards, the sophisticated casting suggesting they were supplied by a commercial ironworks. When the building closed in 1981, it was the most complete and best preserved of all the dockyard chapels. Towards the centre of the yard is Holl's offices for the senior dockyard officials, completed towards the end of 1809 and little altered since.

While the chapel and offices were under construction, other buildings and engineering works were under way or being planned to improve the dockyard's warship building and repair capacity. Work began in 1806 on a new and much larger smithery to replace one described as old, patched, inadequate, leaky and badly planned. The new No. 1 Smithery was enlarged later on several occasions, but the twin lodges and much of the outer walls are original. Chatham's specialisation as a shipbuilding yard made it the almost inevitable choice in 1812 to locate Marc Brunel's steam sawmills, with their extraordinary and possibly unique combination of canal tunnel used to float tree trunks from the southern mast pond to a vertical elliptical shaft alongside the mill. Here a crane on an overhead railway raised and then carried the logs to the stacking yard before returning them to the mill's circular saws. The mechanical side of all this was very largely Brunel, but Holl was responsible for the overall external design of the mill building, which started work in 1814. Two years later he collaborated with John Rennie on the design of the fire-proof twin engine and boiler house for the steam pumps for Rennie's new dry dock, now No. 3 Dock and the first stepped stone dock at the yard. Holl's final contribution came in 1817 with his Lead and Paint Mills, a building unique to Chatham. The flammable contents and processes associated with paint production account for Holl making the building

The fireproof Lead and Paint Mills designed by Holl and constructed between 1817 and 1819. The building contained a lead furnace, rolling mill, grinding mills for paint pigment, and a stove for boiling oil. The adjustable frames, which still remain on the upper floor, were used to stretch canvas prior to painting.

[The National Archives]

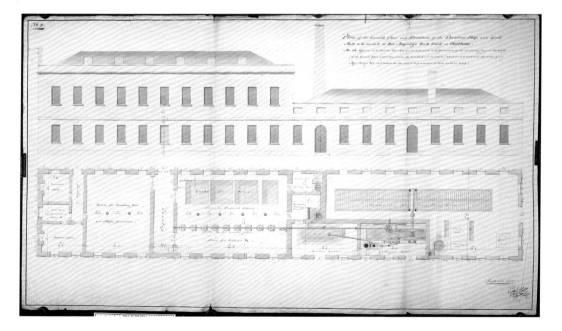

fireproof using his usual combination of cast and wrought iron structural members, metal doors and York stone paving for the floors. On the ground floor a steam engine powered a lead rolling machine for sheet lead and a series of mills for grinding paint colours; oil was kept in tanks below floor level, while on the top floor canvas needing painting was stretched on the still-extant adjustable metal frames.

Elevation of the Front, for the new proposed Steam Engine for Extracting the Water from the Docks at the Royal Dock Yard at Chatham.

Plan.

An unrealised design for the pumping station for the new No. 3 Dock designed by Rennie in 1816. This splendid Gothic alternative may have been inspired by the dockyard Main Gate and the Officers' Terrace of a century earlier.

[The National Archives]

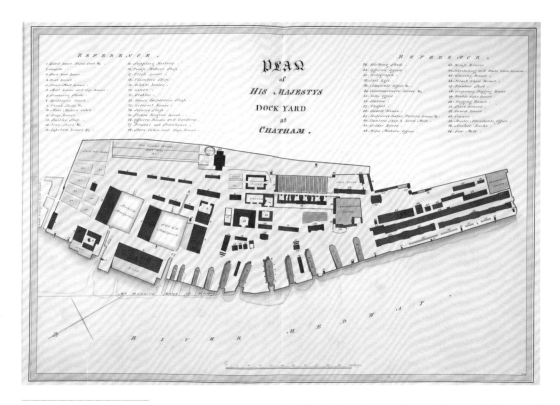

Chatham Dockyard in 1831. Most
of the buildings here still remain.
On the left is the foreshore area
of the Medway that would be
reclaimed to extend the yard and
provide space for building slips 3–7
in the next quarter century.
[© The British Library Board
(Add 21139 f.6)]

Between 1815 and 1860 the riverfront at the northern end of the yard
acquired its present configuration, reflecting a series of almost continuous
improvements. The early ones involved both Rennie and Holl, notably in
the construction of No. 3 Dock and the associated steam pumping station.
No. 2 Dock was rebuilt and enlarged, and in the late 1830s construction
began on the five large building slips. In 1817 the Admiralty had ordered
all such slips to be roofed after being greatly impressed by new and
pioneering slip roofs built at Deptford and Woolwich. Sheltering warships
under construction promised significant reduction in the incidence of dry
rot in their hulls. This outstanding group at Chatham, their huge roofs
dominating the surrounding area, marks the apogee and omega of these
tremendous yet graceful structures. They also reflect changes in building
technology from the all-timber No. 3 Slip roof of 1837 to the all-metal
4–7 roofs of 1847–52. Metal warships constructed from the 1860s had no
need for such protection, and this group, along with two timber slip roofs
in Devonport, are the last such survivors in the country still protecting
their slips.

The construction of HMS *Warrior* in 1860, the world's first all-metal
armour-plated warship, inaugurated a revolution in the world's navies,
naval bases and naval warfare. The Royal Navy re-equipped, ordering
sister ships, known as the 'Black Battlefleet' from the colour of their hulls.
At Chatham, this development led directly to the building between 1864
and 1885 of the vast new steam yard for these vessels. This extension
quadrupled the size of the dockyard, with all the essential new metal-
working facilities and dry docks ranged alongside three huge basins

The massive timber roof of 1837 over No. 3 Slip, one of only three such timber structures in the country. This 1984 photograph shows its later covering before the original material and the skylights were reinstated.
[Chatham Historic Dockyard Trust]

Slips 3–7 from the Medway. The all-timber roof of 1837 to No. 3 Slip on the right was followed some ten years later by the all-metal roofs of slips 4–6. The range was completed in 1852 by Greene's sophisticated No. 7 Slip roof of 1852. This 1982 photograph shows the range before conservation by the Chatham Historic Dockyard Trust.
[Jonathon Coad collection]

formed from St Mary's Creek. Completion of these works shifted the focus of activities away from the older dockyard. This remained in use, fortunately suffering only minor damage in the Second World War, but was to see little new development before the closure of the entire base in 1984.

The buildings and engineering workshops of Chatham Historic Dockyard are unique in their completeness, an unparalleled collection reflecting the requirements of the sailing navy. Fortuitously, and an added bonus helping set the dockyard in the wider naval context, this area also retains important links to the Black Battlefleet and the 20th-century Royal Navy. HMS *Warrior* had been built by the Thames Ironworks, a private shipyard at Blackwall. The Admiralty, determined that naval bases must acquire the skills to build and maintain similar ships, selected Chatham as the pioneer Royal dockyard to construct the second ironclad, HMS *Achilles*. Her keel was laid in No. 2 Dock in 1861. Alongside, a substantial iron-framed metal-clad workshop was constructed with a smithery and equipment for bending the massive angle irons forming the frame of *Achilles*. This building still stands by the dock, both witnesses to the adaptability of the Victorian shipwrights learning new metalworking trades and skills.

Growth in size of iron and, later, steel warships meant that by 1900 the group of covered slips was increasingly used for storage with only No. 7 Slip still in regular use. In 1908, C17, the first Royal Navy submarine to be constructed in a Royal dockyard, was built here. Submarines could be easily accommodated on the slip, while its roof and walls shielded the vessels from prying eyes. C17 was to be followed by a further 57 submarines built and launched here, the last in 1966. No other dockyard could remotely rival this total for these most feared of 20th-century naval vessels. Fittingly, the fifty-fifth and last Chatham-built submarine for the Royal Navy, HMS *Ocelot*, is permanently berthed nearby in No. 3 dry dock, within sight of No. 1 Smithery which, together with the adjacent and long-demolished No. 2 Smithery, were last active contributing to the submarine-building programme.

High boundary walls and 20th-century security restrictions meant that few people outside naval bases were aware of the wealth of historic buildings and engineering works that they contained, many of which were unique to the dockyards. One of the first to realise the historic

HMS *Achilles*, the first armoured metal warship to be built in a Royal dockyard in the early stages of construction, No. 2 Dock in 1860–1. The yard's first machine shop can be seen on the left. Eight of the 14 armoured warships built in the royal dockyards over the next ten years were constructed here at Chatham.

[Chatham Historic Dockyard Trust]

Slips 3–7 had all been designed for wooden warships of the sailing navy. Between 1907 and 1966, 6 and 7 slips were used to construct 57 submarines. Here shipwrights are 'knocking up the wedges' prior to the launch of one of the last O-class submarines.
[Chatham Historic Dockyard Trust]

importance of the old heart of Chatham Dockyard was the Australian, Admiral John Crace (1887–1968), commander of the Australian squadron at the Battle of the Coral Sea in 1942, who went on to hold the post of Admiral Superintendent of the Medway Yard until 1946. He wrote and published a short history of the dockyard and is also credited with arranging for small enamel plaques to be attached to the older buildings, recording their original names and dates of construction. A number of these remain *in situ*. In 1966 Arnold Taylor, then Chief Inspector of Ancient Monuments at the Ministry of Public Building and Works (later Department of the Environment), authorised an assessment of the historic importance of buildings and engineering works in the three operational naval bases of Chatham, Portsmouth and Devonport and the scheduling of those considered to be of 'national importance' under the terms of the Ancient Monuments legislation. The ongoing research stemming from the assessment brought to a wider and influential audience that the three operational naval bases all contained buildings and engineering works of very considerable interest and in some cases of outstanding historic, architectural or industrial significance. What clearly stood out was the near totality of survival in the old heart of Chatham yard of virtually all the component parts of a Georgian and early Victorian dockyard. This information came at a crucial time when the Ministry of Defence (MoD) was considering the future of its naval bases and as yet had no conservation policies of its own to guide redevelopment proposals.

The first test of resolve came in a minor way in 1972 when the MoD put forward proposals to demolish the two disused timber seasoning sheds at Chatham in favour of a car park. In an unprecedented move, one driven by an appreciation of the need to preserve the totality of the historic estate at Chatham, the Ancient Monuments Board for England, an independent but powerful body who advised the Minister of Public Building and Works, recommended that the two structures should be taken into guardianship by the State, joining a distinguished national collection that included Rochester and Upnor castles. Once in guardianship and after conservation, one of the seasoning sheds once again was used to season timber, this time for repairing the State's historic buildings. In 1975 an internal MoD report suggested that Chatham Naval Base could be reduced in size and the pre-1860 dockyard disposed of. Nothing came of this suggestion, but it did add to rising uncertainty about the future of the base at a time when there was growing alarm in conservation circles about the state and fate of historic buildings in Woolwich Arsenal and in the former Sheerness and Pembroke dockyards. In 1974 Nos 1 and 2 smitheries were closed, and two years later the MoD sought to demolish them. Permission to demolish the scheduled No. 1 Smithery was refused. No. 2 Smithery was the younger building, but in a worse state of repair. It did, however, contain a great deal of historic equipment, much of it originating from its neighbour. By agreement this was transferred to store in No. 1 Smithery and what was then still an uncertain future. This was to provide a useful precedent a few years later.

In what proved a prescient move in the autumn of 1980, the Ancient Monuments Board for England appointed a small panel of its members chaired by Dr Basil Greenhill, then director of the National Maritime Museum. The panel's remit was 'To inspect the Scheduled Monuments in the three naval bases of Chatham, Portsmouth and Devonport, to report on their significance, present condition and future use, to assess priorities; and to make recommendations'. Preparation of the report was completed in May 1981, just a month before the Defence Secretary announced that Chatham Naval Base would close in 1984. The panel's report pulled no punches: 'The great ancient monuments in the Royal Dockyards cannot be allowed to deteriorate further through neglect. Positive decisions must be taken now to secure the future of these buildings and engineering works or accept their loss'.

The protracted official negotiations that led to the announcement of the setting up of the Chatham Historic Dockyard Trust just before Christmas 1983 and an endowment of £11 million – then the largest-ever government grant for building conservation – are described elsewhere. This successful outcome had by no means been certain, and it was during this time when the dockyard's future was in limbo that the last piece of the jigsaw was put in place, providing final justification for the title of this chapter.

Part of the collection of machinery and equipment salvaged from the 19th-century extension of the naval base in 1982/83 and stored in No. 1 Smithery.
[Chatham Historic Dockyard Trust]

Closing a major naval base was a huge and lengthy operation. Buildings had to be emptied of their contents, the latter to be packed and sent to other naval bases, sold, scrapped or in some cases simply burned. This operation was a magnet for scrap metal dealers and others. There were concerns not just that important items of historic equipment might be lost through ignorance of their existence or their historic value, but that other equipment, not necessarily of intrinsic historic interest but important for its contribution to the sense of place – such as dockside cranes – would be scrapped.

Finding and collecting the smaller items of historic interest such as hand tools, models, small pieces of machinery and equipment, personal items and similar that might lurk in drawers, cupboards and abandoned storerooms and workshops was undertaken with skill by the newly formed Chatham Dockyard Historical Society. The great majority of the members then were working in the naval base and generally knew the whereabouts of such historically valuable items. Rear-Admiral George Brewer, the Flag Officer, allowed use of the empty Lead and Paint Mills where a vast and varied collection was assembled and is now displayed in the dockyard museum in the Fitted Rigging House.

The immediate problem of saving larger pieces of historic equipment, from steam hammers to giant metal presses, and engines and rolling stock from the dockyard railway, along with items important for their 'sense of place', owes much to an invaluable initiative by the MoD. It agreed that such items identified and selected in a joint survey by the Inspectorate of Ancient Monuments and the National Maritime Museum would be set

Dockyard steam cranes collected
and stored on Anchor Wharf in
1982.
[Chatham Historic Dockyard Trust]

aside in a 'holding account' for a possible future Trust. If the latter did not materialise, the collection would be disposed of. The National Maritime Museum additionally gave a temporary safe home to the contents of the dockyard plans room, while in a further and helpful move the MoD channelled additional orders to the Ropery to extend its operation and hopefully attract a commercial operator. News of these various rescue operations was well received within the naval base and led to further items of interest being volunteered for the 'set aside' collection.

All this ensured that the Chatham Historic Dockyard Trust inherited not just buildings and engineering works but, hugely importantly, also much of the historic machinery, tools and equipment so crucial for a fuller understanding and appreciation of how this vast industrial enterprise

Steam hammers, probably
originally in No. 1 Smithery, in the
Boiler Shop in the 19th-century
extension where they had been
driven by compressed air. These
were carefully dismantled and
set aside.
[Jonathon Coad collection]

Restored Second World War
dockyard locomotive *Ajax* and
wagons pass the covered slips
in 2018.
[Chatham Historic Dockyard Trust]

A mobile canteen donated to the dockyard by the people of Guelph and Wellington County in Ontario during the Second World War. [Record photograph, Chatham Historic Dockyard Trust]

A giant set of plate bending rolls purchased by the Admiralty in 1913. Now displayed in the historic dockyard they are a powerful reminder that Chatham continued as a major naval base until closure in 1984.
[Chatham Historic Dockyard Trust]

served the Royal Navy. In this respect, Chatham Historic Dockyard is unique among its peers. Its immediate local setting also owes much to the yard's existence and aids our understanding of its role and early importance to the State. Just across the Medway, Upnor Castle stands guard, built in the first years of Queen Elizabeth I's reign to defend the fleet anchorage and new dockyard and later to be at the heart of the Navy's ordnance depot here. The dockyard's continuing importance in the 18th century is attested by the great bastioned defences of the Chatham Lines, among the best preserved of their type, begun in 1755 to protect Chatham from overland attack and still crowning the high ground overlooking the dockyard. Nearby is Brompton Barracks, since 1812 home of the Royal Engineers, whose professional training and skills were widely employed not only in fortifications but also in the civil and structural engineering increasingly essential in the Royal dockyards. There is no more telling place to comprehend the formidable investment made by successive governments in the defence of the realm and the centrality of the Royal Navy to that during this great Age of Sail.

Notes

1   TNA ADM/7/660 13.7.1773.
2   TNA ADM/7/662 4.6.1775.

References

Coad, J G 1969 'Chatham Ropeyard'. *Post-Medieval Archaeology* **3**, 143–65

Coad, J G 1982 'Historic Architecture of Chatham Dockyard, 1700–1850'. *Mariner's Mirror* **68**.2, 133–88

Coad, J G 1989 *The Royal Dockyards 1690–1850*. Aldershot: Scolar Press

Coad, J G 2011 'Indifference, Destruction, Appreciation, Conservation: A Century of Changing Attitudes to Historic Buildings in British Naval Bases'. *Mariner's Mirror* **97**.1, 314–43

Coad, J G 2013 *Support for the Fleet. Architecture and Engineering of the Royal Navy's Bases 1700–1914*. Swindon: English Heritage

Kendall, P 2012 *The Royal Engineers at Chatham 1750–2012*. Swindon: English Heritage

MacDougall, P 2009 *Chatham Dockyard 1815–1865*. London: The Navy Records Society, Vol. 154

4 The challenge of the future

Paul Hudson

On 1 April 1984, the former naval base[1] at Chatham started a new life on its own without the Royal Navy, which had been the simple reason for its existence. Few of us who were involved at that time could have imagined what this huge site might become, though we might well have had high hopes for the preservation and development of the most historic southern part of the dockyard, even then regarded as the most complete survival of a Georgian naval dockyard in existence.

As is well known, the decision to close Chatham naval base was announced to the House of Commons on 25 June 1981 by John (later Sir) Nott, Secretary of State for Defence at the time. This was following a review of naval defences and, as a consequence, what support in the form of shore naval bases the Navy might need in the future. Did the Navy really need full-scale dockyards in Devonport, Portsmouth, Rosyth and Chatham? Fears about the future of Chatham had been expressed for some years though. From the conclusion of the submarine-building programme in 1968, the dockyard's principal task had been the major refitting and modernisation of the Navy's fleet submarines and certain classes of frigates. Some comfort had been taken from the substantial investment in the nuclear submarine refuelling centre as indicating a guarantee of Chatham's future, a view shared by the senior naval staff at Chatham. It was not to be, however, and there was nothing to cushion the blow when closure was announced, a decision met with resignation rather than surprise.

So, while the role of both Devonport and Portsmouth dockyards was to be sharply reduced, the decision was to close Chatham entirely by 1984. That at least meant there were three years in which to think about what new future the naval base might hold, but there was no getting away from the fact that this was a looming catastrophe for the Medway towns. The 1980s were the high point of economic restructuring, with many basic industries in Kent as elsewhere closing and having to adapt to radically changing circumstances. North Kent had already seen the closure of the BP oil refinery at the mouth of the Medway on the Isle of Grain, and the progressive closure of papermaking, chalk extraction and cement manufacture nearby in Kent Thameside.

But the closure of Chatham naval base was in a different league. Not only had the dockyard been in existence for over 400 years, but it was in many respects the heart of the Medway towns physically, economically and culturally. It had been unequivocally the mainspring of the Medway towns' economy for at least the last century, and at its peak during the Second World War had provided over 17,000 jobs directly, let alone the huge range of local businesses that depended upon the dockyard for their order book. Even at the closure announcement in 1981, the dockyard still employed perhaps 6,500 local people, and widely publicised forecasts at the time were that unemployment rates in the Medway towns would top 25 per cent once it closed.[2]

Nott's axe falls on Chatham:
Chatham *Evening Post* special
edition cover Friday 26 June 1981.
[Chatham Historic Dockyard Trust]

Not surprisingly, the initial response was to seek to persuade the government to reverse its decision, and energetic campaigns were fought by the local MPs Peggy Fenner and Sir Freddy Burden, as well as the local press. But it soon became clear that the government was not for moving, and the best that could be hoped for was some form of assistance to cushion the blow. The challenges that Chatham naval base faced were colossal. Not only was its sheer scale enormous, covering 650 acres, paradoxically it was also insulated from the middle of the urban area within which it was set. Its very advantage, from a security point of view, of being located in a sharp bend of the Medway with the land boundary secured by a high brick wall breached by just three entrances, meant that it was impossible simply to absorb it directly into the urban structure. Added to that, the growing likelihood of its eventual closure meant that investment in utilities and services had been kept to a minimum in recent years, and there was widespread ground contamination, particularly on St Mary's Island from years of heavy industrial activity.

From an administrative point of view, at that time the Medway towns were governed by two district councils: the City of Rochester-upon-Medway covering the western side of the urban area, and Gillingham Borough Council, in whose area the vast majority of the Chatham naval base lay. Neither council saw the immediate priority as thinking too much about the future possibilities that this huge site might represent for the Medway towns, but understandably wanted to concentrate on the immediate response for the local economy of closure of the Medway towns' largest employer. So, at that point, what turned out to be a farsighted proposal was suggested by the then county planning officer for Kent, Harry Deakin. This was that, at the very least, local government as a whole needed to understand as much as possible about the current state of the dockyard, and therefore commissioned his department to prepare a number of appraisals and studies of the whole naval base in order to provide a basis for future decisions.

He appointed me as the head of a recently established economic development unit in Kent County Council's planning department to lead a team of planners and architects for this purpose. Harry Deakin personally made the appropriate contacts with bodies such as the National Maritime Museum and its then director Dr Basil Greenhill, and those experts in the maritime conservation field including Jonathan Coad[3] and Neil Cossons[4] to make sure that the significance of Chatham was properly

The Falklands Crisis took place the year after the dockyard's closure was announced. HMS *Endurance*, the Chatham-based Antarctic Patrol vessel, returned to Chatham on 20 August 1982 to a rapturous welcome.
[Chatham Historic Dockyard Trust]

Harry Deakin, Kent County Council
Planning Officer 1974–88.
[Paul Hudson Collection]

Cover of the 1981 Planning
Appraisal for the historic dockyard.
[Chatham Historic Dockyard Trust]

21 June 1983, HMS *Hermione*,
the last warship to be refitted at
Chatham departs, a banner on her
guardrails proclaiming 'Last One,
Best One'.
[Chatham Historic Dockyard Trust]

understood and accurately described. The report dealing with what was termed 'the historic dockyard' was the first one of the series and was produced in November 1981. It was followed by appraisals of the rest of the naval base carried out in early 1982 jointly with the two district councils. It is fair to say that they formed the basis of the approach taken by Kent County Council, Rochester-upon-Medway City Council and Gillingham Borough Council in negotiations with the central government departments involved over the succeeding three years, with the emphasis on highlighting the opportunities as well as the problems.

However, it is the planning appraisal of the historic dockyard which is of most concern to this chapter. In his introduction to the report, Harry Deakin stated that 'the historic dockyard offers a unique combination of circumstances where the needs of conservation and those of commerce and employment can each support the other, and I hope that the opportunity to realise the potential now presented will not be missed'. Forty years on and no one has put it better. Indeed, it is remarkable how much of the initial thinking in the planning appraisal remains accurate and as relevant today as when it was put together.

Even before the closure of Chatham naval base was announced and the interest of the local authorities in its future then stimulated, there had been recognition of the significance of the range of Georgian naval buildings. Their very existence as a comprehensive group was a precious asset, despite the inevitable changes and adaptations that the buildings and structures had witnessed over many years. In May 1981, the Ancient Monuments Directorate of the then Department of the Environment (DoE) had published a report about the significance, condition and future uses of Scheduled Monuments in the Royal dockyards, including Chatham as the only one to survive intact. It argued that urgent action was required to prevent further deterioration of several important buildings, piecemeal

Pembroke Gate: The final closure of the Dockyard gates, 31 March 1984. The mayors of both Gillingham and Rochester look on, while Sir Steuart Pringle holds a presentation casket wishing Chatham Historic Dockyard Trust future success.

Aerial view of the dockyard c 1981–83. The density of more modern buildings close to the north mast pond is clearly visible, including the main office block which the MoD attempted to pass on to the Regional Health Authority as part of a piecemeal sell-off of individual buildings and structures.
[Chatham Historic Dockyard Trust]

break-up of the historic group of buildings, and to prevent the random loss of machinery and equipment.

The report in fact reflected a recent proposal from the Navy itself that the historic area could be separated from the rest of the dockyard as it no longer had much need for this collection of now essentially heritage buildings and structures. It also proposed the establishment of a trust

to take on the task. Timing is everything: in June 1981, shortly after the completion of this report, the government announced the progressive rundown of the whole naval base at Chatham, leading to complete closure by 1984.

Essentially, the historic dockyard at Chatham had survived as a group of over 100 buildings and structures, 47 of them Scheduled Monuments, covering the southern 80 acres of Chatham Dockyard, because of the ability to expand dockyard activities onto fresh land to the north rather than redevelop the existing estate. Jonathan Coad's work, for example his seminal article in the *Mariner's Mirror* in May 1982, had already alerted many in the conservation field to the importance of this enclave. The fact that it was about to be closed and therefore its future cast in doubt added to fears about its long-term protection and survival, let alone what beneficial new uses this special group of dockyard buildings and structures could be put towards.

Kent County Council's 1981 planning appraisal underlined that the historic dockyard was unique, and should be conserved as an enclosed and open-air maritime museum. But it also recognised that this use alone would be unlikely to make full use of the site or sustain the cost of preserving all the structures of historic importance. The aim therefore must be to achieve a sympathetic superimposition of mixed activities (which might include residential, industrial and commercial uses) on the museum role of the historic dockyard.

However, the appraisal also recognised a number of underlying problems which would need to be overcome:

- Some buildings, notably the Ropery, accommodated activities which remained substantially unchanged since the 18th century; these buildings not only contributed architecturally to the external appreciation of the historic dockyard, but housed processes which are themselves living history. The priority would be to try to keep the uses of such buildings as intact as possible, but on a new commercial footing.
- Others, like the Mould Loft, had changed their use but retained an internal structure of historic interest which any future use should seek to preserve.
- Another group of buildings, such as the Anchor Wharf Stores and Fitted Rigging House, the dry docks and covered slips, were on a massive scale, and perhaps trying to reuse them for some form of shipbuilding facilities was a hopeful possibility.
- But there were several examples of buildings such as the Smithery which were virtually derelict at the time the appraisal was carried out and for them the challenge was to find an appropriate alternative use while maintaining the external appearance of the building.
- In many cases, the objective of retaining some degree of public access to what would be buildings in private commercial use in order to maintain the museum function of the whole historic dockyard would represent an ongoing tension.

The planning appraisal also recognised – even at the outset – that a concerted effort would be needed to maintain the overall environment and appearance of the historic dockyard and its maritime and naval purpose. The detail which was apparent even in 1981 – ranging from mooring rings along the riverside wall, bollards and capstans alongside the dry docks, flagpoles beside the old harbourmaster's office and the captain of the dockyard's house, pulley blocks above loading doors on the Fitted Rigging House and dockyard railway lines – although not all of intrinsic historic interest contributed substantially to the atmosphere of the historic dockyard. It was obvious that as closure loomed and interest waned, these important details were vulnerable to casual removal as being of little importance. Fortunately for Chatham, there was a long-standing Dockyard Historical Society which assumed responsibility for collecting a wide range of objects and artefacts which would almost certainly have been lost.[5]

The broader context of the historic dockyard was noted, given that the views across the River Medway to modern industrial development on the Frindsbury peninsular were visually unattractive, in evident contrast to the views back towards the historic dockyard. Longer-distance views towards Rochester Cathedral and the castle were particularly important to retain in maintaining the overall place of the historic dockyard in the Medway towns.

Conservation, land-use and management decisions therefore needed to be taken within an overall framework and to be subject to a design brief. A huge effort would be needed to seek out and encourage appropriate industrial and maritime uses, which themselves should complement the character of the historic dockyard. Perhaps most importantly, the planning appraisal stressed that the historic area should be retained under a single ownership, and that this issue should be resolved urgently. Suggested options were through a statutory mechanism such as an urban development corporation, a popular regeneration vehicle of the time, a local government committee, or a purpose-built trust, though from the outset the latter was the preferred approach.

The significance of this was that, at the time, the prevailing approach of the Ministry of Defence (MoD) and the government's Property Service Agency (PSA), responsible for disposal of the naval base, was to convey individual buildings and spaces as interest and demand arose, without much regard for maintaining the overall integrity of the dockyard. But such was the impact of dockyard closure on the local economy that any expression of interest by potential entrepreneurs and developers needing buildings or spaces was heartily welcomed. In this context, the county council's view that such speculative proposals for any part of the naval base should be resisted unless they fitted within the framework of a comprehensive overall plan was not received very sympathetically locally.

Nonetheless, the county council stuck to its resolve that one of the biggest advantages the naval base as a whole offered for the future was the simple point that it was in single ownership, and that splitting it up into unrelated parcels to meet a range of possible development interests was unlikely to offer the best overall future. Also, the self-contained nature of the services and utilities, which were mostly separated from and independent of those in the Medway towns as a whole, militated against simple disposal of individual buildings. The particular needs and circumstances of the historic dockyard were therefore just a microcosm of the strategic approach to the redevelopment of the naval base as a whole.

In any event, much bigger decisions were needed before the questions of such future redevelopment could be properly tackled. Top of the agenda for most people was to radically improve physical, and in particular vehicular, access to the whole naval base estate. While tearing down the walls was never appropriate for the historic dockyard, it certainly became the approach conceptually, if not figuratively, in relation to the rest of the naval base. One of the biggest achievements in due course was the opening in 1996 of a new tunnel under the Medway as a joint venture between the county council as highway authority and the Rochester Bridge Trust, linking the very centre of the naval base directly to the rest of the urban area and, more importantly, to the strategic road network through new link roads in both directions to the M2.[6] Added to that was the need to comprehensively deal with the substantial contamination left on many parts of the more modern parts of the naval base, particularly St Mary's Island, in order to enable this to be properly prepared for future development.

For the historic dockyard, the principal decision about maintaining its overall integrity was perhaps somewhat easier, given the recognition that this was a group of buildings which were no longer of direct value to the modern Navy. Even though its historic heart might well lie there, for example in the form of its oldest intact naval building, Medway (Commissioners) House, the historic dockyard was essentially a physical appendix to the majority of the naval base, and which could be fairly readily separated from it. Moreover, the gradually accepted area embracing the historic dockyard was entirely in the Rochester-upon-Medway City Council area, which made negotiations about its future uses rather easier to handle.

Having raised the planning and conservation importance of the historic dockyard within Kent, the next target was to persuade the government of the need to establish an appropriate mechanism or organisation to realise the potential. As is so often the case with understanding the evolution of major decisions, the happy circumstance of the right people being in the right position at the right time becomes very apparent with the passage of time. In the case of Chatham, this was the role played by John Spence, a senior Kent county councillor, and Robert (Bobby) Neame, the leader of Kent County Council at that time.

John Spence had begun his own professional career in Chatham Dockyard and was on the staff of Flag Officer Medway, so therefore knew it intimately. At the same time, he was reaching the peak of his career in local government, having served as a member of Gillingham Borough Council, and then representing the Medway towns on Kent County Council. He was during this period variously chairman of Kent County Council's finance committee, chairman of the Kent Police Authority, and was playing a prominent role in representing local government interests nationally on the Association of County Councils. Politically, he was very close to Bobby Neame, who himself needed little persuasion of the strategic opportunity that redevelopment of the Chatham naval base could offer, and the particular role that the historic dockyard itself could play within that.

This was a set of circumstances where the professional interests and understanding of Kent County Council chief officers such as county planning officer Harry Deakin and chief executive Bill Jackson confidently matched the political priorities that senior county councillors such as John Spence and Bobby Neame attached to ensuring a successful outcome. It is not too fanciful to say that without the strategic grasp of the issues that perhaps only the county council could undertake in bringing together the two district councils in negotiations with central government, the eventual outcome for the historic dockyard, and indeed the naval base as a whole, would have been very different.

The first task in this endeavour was to persuade the government to take the future of the historic dockyard seriously once the Navy left in 1984. After all, the government was the landowner in the form of the MoD. Many organisations had made representations to Michael Heseltine, the Secretary of State for Environment at the time, about the future of the Scheduled Monuments within the historic dockyard, but as noted above, the prevailing ethos of the PSA at the time was simply to dispose of unwanted assets to the highest bidder. Partly to help neutralise this approach, the county council realised that it was important to bind the government into a shared view of the future.

Accordingly, Kent County Council's chief executive lobbied the permanent secretary of the DoE to jointly commission and pay for a consultant's study of the historic dockyard. This was agreed in February 1982 following a visit to Chatham by Michael Heseltine when he made a personal commitment to maintain the integrity of the dockyard. The slight discomfort in these arrangements was that the DoE's representative on the steering group was to be the deputy chief executive of the PSA.

A study was indeed commissioned in April 1982 from a multidisciplinary team of consultants led by architects Lewis Wilson and Hugh Womersley, and chartered surveyors Richard Ellis. This was a high-profile appointment from prestigious professional consultants and as much as anything else was designed

- to provide credibility and weight to both the importance of the historic dockyard as a group of listed buildings and Scheduled Monuments;
- to endorse the options for realising the future development potential of the historic dockyard as a museum and combination of commercial activities; but
- crucially, to provide some financial perspective on the challenges of maintaining the buildings.

Plainly, the government's interest was to reduce its liabilities for maintaining a large number of buildings of acknowledged acute conservation significance as the defence need for them was shortly to cease. Not surprisingly, the MoD considered it would have little continuing responsibility as its interests were at an end and saw no reason to spend any more money on the buildings than was absolutely essential. At the same time, the DoE, while endorsing the conservation significance of the dockyard, had few resources to underpin future liabilities which it felt were not its responsibility, particularly as they had arisen through years of under-investment by another government department.

Nonetheless, when published in October 1982, the Wilson Womersley/Richard Ellis report generally endorsed Kent County Council's planning appraisal of November 1981 and provided a solid foundation for the next steps:

1   The future for the historic dockyard was seen in bringing it to life through a mix of complementary uses, particularly tourism. The alternative of regarding the dockyard as just a museum was specifically rejected. There was the basis for the creation of an environment of high quality in the historic dockyard, arising from the site itself and the superb collection of buildings.

2   Future uses for many of the buildings were reasonably obvious, particularly those already in residential and office use. The main problems would occur with those very special buildings which give the historic dockyard its unique character, such as the covered slips and docks, the Smithery and the massive Anchor Wharf Stores fronting the River Medway.

3   Apart from possible new housing developments at the northern end of the historic dockyard and on the site of the south mast pond, the consultants were gloomy about the prospects for industry, offices, retail or hotel uses.

4   Market demand for most of the proposed uses was assessed as low, and their financial viability limited. Some of the proposed uses, such as residential and offices, would generate income, but this would not be sufficient to outweigh the costs.

5   It was noted that about £4 million worth of work was proposed by the PSA on reroofing the Officers' Terrace, Ropery and covered slips, and this was assumed to be completed by 1984.

6   The net deficit, on a once-and-for-all capital endowment basis (including the capitalisation of annual maintenance), was estimated at about £9.75 million, assuming the PSA's repair programme was completed by 1984. Over £5.5 million of this was for environmental improvements, establishment costs, new tourist displays and management running costs.

7   Unified ownership of the historic dockyard was strongly recommended as essential, and a trust, possibly with charitable status, proposed as the best type of organisation to direct and finance the operation. Private-sector finance could be introduced for certain sites and buildings.

Frankly, the Wilson Womersley/Richard Ellis report did not add much to the knowledge about the importance of individual buildings. Its value was in endorsing the significance of the historic dockyard as an entity,[7] providing an estimate of the condition and repair costs associated with each building and structure, and making a strong case for the establishment of a purpose-built organisation. This would assume responsibility for the historic dockyard, all its buildings and artefacts, and secure its future preservation and development as both a museum and tourist attraction, supported by appropriate commercial development to provide income.

The report assessed the immediate liability for bringing the buildings into a reasonable state of repair, often little more than basic windproof and watertight measures, and proposed a number of priorities about which buildings should be attended to first.[8] In the light of this, the view of ministers and senior officials was that establishing a purpose-built form of organisation to take responsibility for the historic dockyard was itself fairly straightforward. But unless it had a substantial endowment at the outset and a fighting chance of securing the necessary resources, the prospects of adequately dealing with the challenges of continuing maintenance of historic buildings would be limited.

That remained the position from the publication of the Wilson Womersley/Richard Ellis study in late 1982 through 1983, until the eventual establishment of the Chatham Historic Dockyard Trust (CHDT) on the eve of the Navy's departure from Chatham at the end of March 1984. But before then, many discussions took place at official and ministerial level to resolve difficulties about setting it up. To the county council it appeared that the basic problem was a disagreement between the two departments headed by Michael Heseltine (now at the MoD) and Patrick Jenkin (at the DoE) about where responsibility properly lay to meet the funding requirements. The expectation was that there would be a joint announcement from them, and a particular milestone anticipated for this was 30 September 1983, when the major ceremony marking the formal departure of the Port Admiral and hence the Royal Navy from Chatham took place. But although Admiral Bill Higgins expressed great confidence about the future for the historic dockyard, he stopped short of any such announcement, which was consequently interpreted locally as an ominous sign.

John Spence and Bobby Neame had been in regular discussions with the government throughout 1983, and became increasingly alarmed at what appeared to be lack of progress, including a disinclination on the part of Prime Minister Margaret Thatcher to intervene. Because it appeared that a mechanism for releasing funding was at the root of the problem, they decided to meet Peter Rees, who at the time was Chief Secretary at the Treasury.[9] This meeting took place on 16 November 1983 and plainly had the desired effect, as an announcement was made in the House of Commons immediately before Christmas 1983 that a trust for the historic dockyard would be established to take over the freehold of the site from the MoD, sponsored by the two secretaries of state (who indeed remain formal members of the CHDT to this day).

The first meeting of the CHDT (the Trust) was held in the MoD in Whitehall in the afternoon following the final closure of the naval base that morning on 30 March 1984. Its first chairman and chief executive was Lt Gen Sir Steuart Pringle, recently retired as Commandant General of the Royal Marines. The other trustees appointed to the board were
- The Hon Anthony Cayzer, deputy chairman
- Mr Christopher Wates[10]
- Mr John Spence
- Mr Leonard Manasseh
- Mr Robert Huskisson
- The Rt Hon Earl Ferrars

1984 – The Trust's first board of trustees pictured outside Commissioners House. Left to right: Robert Huskisson, Leonard Manasseh, Anthony Cayzer (deputy chairman), Sir Steuart Pringle (chairman and chief executive), John Spence, Earl Ferrars, Christopher Wates.
[Chatham Historic Dockyard Trust]

On its initial establishment, the Trust had no staff apart from one or two former dockyard employees who remained on the payroll of the PSA to provide administrative and maintenance support. Indeed, such was the county council's commitment to helping the Trust get established that the county secretary, Bill Hopkin, acted as the company secretary for the first few months. And at a more practical level, members of staff from the planning department (particularly Rod Macleod, who had been largely responsible for the preparation of the planning appraisal some 18 months earlier) were seconded to the Trust.

The Trust's first task, therefore, was to build an organisation. Sir Steuart Pringle saw himself as the full-time chief executive as well as being chairman of the board of trustees. This situation continued until the appointment in 1986 of Bruce Robertson, a planner with recent experience of the regeneration of St Katherine Dock in London, as general manager, and who eventually took over the role of chief executive in December 1991.

The Trust was established with an endowment from the government of £11.35 million,[11] representing the minimum sum felt necessary to enable immediate maintenance priorities to be met, and giving the Trust sufficient breathing space to be able to establish commercial ventures to generate sufficient income to secure its long-term future. Although this squared reasonably with the estimate of costs arising from the consultant's study in 1982, the immediate problem for the Trust was that shortly before its establishment, the PSA had let a contract for the reroofing of the quarter-mile-long Ropery at a sum of £3.5 million, which was to be paid from the £11.35 million endowment. This reduced the actual endowment available

The Mast Houses and Mould Loft
clad in metal sheeting in 1984.
[Chatham Historic Dockyard Trust]

to the Trust to £7.85 million. Not surprisingly, the Trust felt this meant there was financially hardly any discretion left so that it was starting its existence with one hand firmly tied behind its back. Nonetheless, it is likely that reroofing the Ropery would have been one of the Trust's own first priorities. The fact that it still looks in extremely sound condition almost 40 years later is a testimony to not only the quality of the work carried out but also a justification for that early decision.

It is easy now to forget the parlous state of many of the buildings and artefacts and the comparatively degraded overall environment in the historic dockyard when the Trust assumed responsibility on 1 April 1984. For many buildings, the immediate future was simply one of locking the door and ensuring the risk of a collapsing roof was removed as far as possible. For some buildings, even this was not a possibility, for example the Smithery, which in later years was simply a shell with hardly any roof and an ever-increasing forest of buddleia taking over the internal spaces. In addition, in the final months before the closure of the dockyard, many artefacts and smaller objects were removed or simply disappeared, whether as souvenirs or transferred to other dockyards. A substantial effort was made by volunteers of the Dockyard Historical Society to retain as many historic objects as possible and store them away safely. The many original artefacts in the museum galleries of the historic dockyard testifies to their success.

Another immediate task facing the Trust was to decide what sort of place Chatham Historic Dockyard should become. There was no shortage of advice, with some identifying potential uses for nearly every building.[12] Others urged that the Trust should take its time: the unique collection of buildings and structures meant it would be all too easy to get it wrong. The common theme was that the overriding priority must be to secure the long-term preservation of the buildings, and to enable future generations

Ropery roof before restoration
works commenced in 1984.
[Chatham Historic Dockyard Trust]

Ropery roof renewed c 1987.
[Chatham Historic Dockyard Trust]

to appreciate that the many different activities and buildings in the Georgian historic dockyard were established for a common purpose: the building and repair of warships.

But within that overarching objective, several different futures were possible. For example:

1 The site could be some form of open-air museum which might aim to recreate a Chatham Historic Dockyard of the 18th and 19th centuries. This could mean all the activities being carried out in as historically authentic a manner as possible to form a visitor attraction, for example the construction of historic ships on the slipways. It would stand the best chance of maximising visitor numbers and income, but would be labour intensive and costly to operate.

2 Museum-related activities could be concentrated in a core part of the site, leaving the peripheral areas much more open to commercial activities. These would need to be within the constraints of the existing buildings and maintaining at least their external appearances and with as few changes as possible. This might enable overall income to the historic dockyard to be generated earlier and transfer the burden of restoration of individual buildings to their users rather than the Trust itself.

3 Should the historic dockyard be open to the public at all times in the same way that, for example, Covent Garden is, or should its security be maintained as an asset and public access restricted? If the future for the historic dockyard was as essentially a museum with a range of other ancillary uses, it would not be easy to allow unrestricted access at all times. Given that the dockyard had been such a restricted site, there was understandably considerable pressure locally that people should be allowed access to a central

Aerial view of the newly completed
Ropery roof – the Anchor Wharf
storehouses lie in front – c 1987.
[Chatham Historic Dockyard Trust]

part of the Medway towns denied to them hitherto.[13] In the early months after closure, there was a considerable risk of vandalism because of the difficulty of maintaining strict security, but fortunately no serious damage occurred. Eventually, the consensus was that maintaining some degree of security was essential in view of the precious nature of the buildings themselves, as well as the overall intention to present the whole site as a paid-entry museum. On that basis, the dockyard wall was one of the site's principal assets, rather than a problem.

4   How best to provide access to the historic dockyard, either through the existing impressive Main Gate, or from a new purpose-built access created at the northern end of Dock Road? Equally difficult issues were how to manage the circulation of vehicles once in the site and the consequential decisions about where car parking for visitors to a new museum should be best located. Using the Main Gate as the principal vehicle access would mean the whole site would suffer from traffic flows and risks to public safety. An early decision therefore was to provide the main public access from the northern end of the site.

5   The historic dockyard had operated as a heavy industrial site with little regard or indeed need for precautions to protect the public from dangerous structures. This extended to obvious hazards such as the dry docks and the south mast pond, but also, because there was little distinction between spaces used by vehicles and pedestrians, the whole historic dockyard was bewildering and therefore a safety hazard to people unfamiliar with the site.

6   A dockyard without any ships was a frequent criticism levelled at the Trust in the early years of its existence. For the dockyard where HMS *Victory* was built, this struck a raw nerve, but the fact remained that when the Navy left, all the ships left with them. The fundamental purpose of Chatham Historic Dockyard gradually emerged that it was not to be the home of a representative range of naval shipping such as at Portsmouth, but to tell the story of how ships themselves were built. Nonetheless, without some examples on hand this ambition was likely to be difficult to achieve, and an early decision was taken to acquire HMS *Gannet* as an example of an 1870s gunboat. This enabled the story to be told of how the Navy protected worldwide shipping trade routes in the heyday of the British Empire. It also helped that the ship was built nearby at Sheerness Dockyard, although it was in a very poor state and itself was the source of a funding campaign supported substantially by Kent County Council and Rochester-upon-Medway City Council to secure its restoration. Subsequently, other important vessels were acquired to enable the historic dockyard to illuminate different phases of its long history: HMS *Cavalier*, representing construction

HM Submarine *Ocelot*, the last warship built at Chatham for the Royal Navy arrives in No. 2 Dock (still in use as a commercial ship repair facility) in 1992.

[Chatham Historic Dockyard Trust]

of warships during the Second World War, and to bring matters more up to date, the submarine HMS *Ocelot*, built at Chatham in 1962.

7   The complete redevelopment of the so-called modern dockyard was recognised early on as of great importance to both the Trust and English Estates as the first body charged with implementing the vision for what was renamed Chatham Maritime. The physical issue was how to treat the boundary between the two sites. The example of Charlestown Navy Yard in Boston was all too clear, that putting up a chain-link fence between a historic enclave and a redevelopment zone would not be the solution. So finding an appropriate range of land uses which would enable the smooth transition between the conservation and museum attributes of the historic dockyard and the purely commercial and residential developments to the north was a major strategic challenge. And so it has remained until the present time.

However, taking time to properly understand the nature of the historic dockyard's assets and the best strategic direction to ensure their future did not chime too well locally. Expectations were high that Chatham Historic Dockyard would become an instant major tourist attraction with

Lord Tebbit, then Chancellor of the Duchy of Lancaster, visited the site in July 1986 to discuss the joint historic dockyard/Chatham Maritime development plans. Left to right: Stephen Pritchard, Ian Parker (both of English Estates), Lord Tebbit, John Spence (trustee) and Bruce Robertson (general manager and later chief executive of CHDT).
[Chatham Historic Dockyard Trust]

little regard for the huge preparatory tasks in creating such an enterprise. Not surprisingly, patience was thin, with a Trust seen to be aloof from the immediate pressing needs of job creation.

Sir Steuart's challenge, therefore, was to seek some early commercial income generators and begin the development of museum galleries as tourist attractions. The board took the view early on that some parts of the historic dockyard could be cleared and redeveloped or indeed sold off entirely as surplus to future needs. Hence, in due course, a self-contained housing scheme was developed between the Smithery and the dockyard wall, requiring the demolition of fairly non-descript former storehouse and office buildings, and the outright disposal of an undeveloped plot known as the Commissioner's Hayfield south of the Lead and Paint Mill.

Charlestown Navy Yard Boston – one way of separating the historic and modern elements.
[Chatham Historic Dockyard Trust]

Though these were understandable decisions in the early years of the Trust in order to generate much-needed revenue as well as encouraging people to live in the dockyard, they demonstrate the difficulty of short-term gain compromising long-term advantage. This is apart from the understandable requirements of residents not always coexisting happily with the historic dockyard as a visitor attraction. As the historic dockyard enters its mature development phase after nearly 40 years of effort, it now runs the risk of running out of space – an unthinkable concept in April 1984.

During the same period, other work was continuing on how to make the best of the rest of the former naval base site. Lessons were drawn from regeneration projects analogous to Chatham such as St Katharine Dock, the Victoria and Alfred waterfront in Cape Town, and most particularly the Charlestown Navy Yard in Boston. This had many parallels with Chatham in having a small historic element within a much larger, more modern naval shipyard. Charlestown had been released from naval use and the site split into a historic and monuments area run by the National Park Service and the rest transferred to an agency of the city council, the Boston Redevelopment Authority. As noted earlier, the crucial lesson for Chatham was that there was a substantial chain-link fence simply dividing the site in two, which underlined the importance of maintaining the unity of the whole Chatham naval base estate as far as possible. Suggestions that Chatham could simply be parcelled up and disposed of to whatever need was most apparent at the time were becoming less attractive, but nonetheless, the example of Charlestown demonstrated the very obvious dangers of not sticking to the fundamental principle.

In order to underline how important this was to both organisations, a joint development plan for Chatham Maritime and Chatham Historic Dockyard was commissioned from consultants Frederick Gibberd Coombes and Partners in March 1985. This in turn spawned detailed planning documents by Rochester-upon-Medway City Council (Chatham Historic Dockyard development and design brief 1986) and jointly with Gillingham Borough Council (joint development brief for Chatham Maritime and Chatham Historic Dockyard 1987).

In the event, the former Chatham naval base was split between three organisations:

- Chatham Historic Dockyard to the CHDT;
- the majority of the modern dockyard and HMS *Pembroke* transferred to the ownership of English Estates, then English Partnerships, subsequently the South East England Development Agency (SEEDA) and currently Homes England; and
- the eastern dock basin and surrounding land transferred to the Medway Ports Authority to run as a commercial port, and this remains the position today under the ownership and management of Peel Ports.

While there is a firm site boundary to provide security for the port operation, there is no such hard fence between the historic dockyard and Chatham Maritime, mainly because the construction of the Medway Tunnel has provided a clear physical separation to make it unnecessary. But that is not to say the land ownerships are entirely logical. When the

Aerial photograph showing the whole dockyard site in 1986.
[Chatham Historic Dockyard Trust]

boundaries of the historic dockyard were finalised in 1984, it was largely to capture the most significant buildings representing the core historic interest rather than a considered attempt to provide a coherent and defensible land holding. As noted earlier, even the Wilson Womersley/ Richard Ellis report of 1982 highlighted that land on both the east and west sides of the north mast pond were excluded from the nominal boundaries of the historic dockyard where they most properly belonged.

The result is that now there are substantial pockets of land owned by Homes England to the south of the Medway Tunnel which are physically and functionally within the historic dockyard. These represent what has come to be termed the interface land. Finding a development solution which satisfies both the commercial ambitions of Homes England and the conservation objectives of providing a suitable setting for the Scheduled Monuments and listed buildings of the historic dockyard has so far proved elusive. The Trust and English Estates/SEEDA/Homes England have striven to maintain a close working relationship throughout the last 35 years, at least recognising that the success of both sides is very much dependent upon the mutual achievement of each neighbour's ambitions. That both organisations have resisted a simple solution of not accepting development which would fail to meet these objectives, but instead holding out for something which will be seen to work properly, is very much to their credit.

It is not the purpose of this chapter to provide a detailed history of the Chatham Historic Dockyard Trust over nearly 40 years, but nonetheless

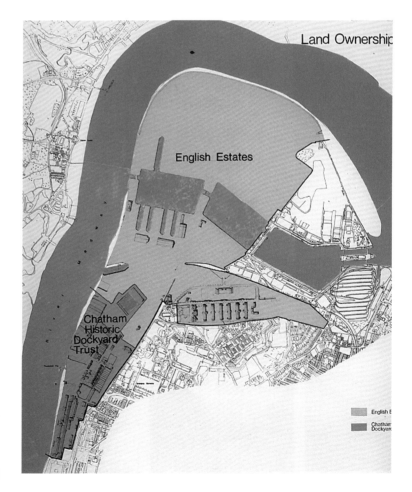

Chatham Dockyard – land-split
map from the 1986 Gibberd
Coombes design study.
[Chatham Historic Dockyard Trust]

it is instructive to look at several major phases which themselves partly reflect the choices open to it at the outset about what sort of place the historic dockyard could be.

The initial challenge was to get the site open to the public, which happened in June 1985 with the modest visitor centre charging for entrance to the historic dockyard. Visitors could see the Ropery in operation by a commercial undertaking, Cosalt, who had taken over with an initial 5-year order book from the MoD. Similarly, Zephyr Flags were in production in the Sail and Colour Loft, with several former dockyard employees now under new management.[14] The beginning of ships at Chatham was started with the arrival of HMS *Gannet* in 1987, and the commencement of a long and expensive restoration programme. At the same time, some commercial developments were introduced, and areas perceived as available for residential development brought into use.

In 1986, the first full year of opening to the public, 14,000 people visited Chatham Historic Dockyard. The main focus thereafter was to get at least one of the historic buildings open as a gallery. This was the award-winning Wooden Walls in the Mast Houses and Mould Loft, which opened in 1990 (and functioned thereafter largely unchanged for 23 years). Additionally, much improved catering for visitors was achieved in the form of the Wheelwrights' restaurant. Accordingly, by 1990 annual visitor numbers had grown to a respectable 95,000. The Trust itself had become a sizeable organisation employing over 100 people (although many of these were temporary seasonal staff), there were 55 commercial tenants, and a start had been made on the new housing development east of the Smithery.

The prospects for finding tenants for some buildings remained intractable, however, and so the Trust took the step of revisiting the prospects for property development. Richard Ellis, part of the consultants team who had carried out the study in 1982, were engaged to look at the opportunities for the problem buildings such as Anchor Wharf, the covered slips and the Lower Boat House. Their conclusions were not encouraging.

Although over £2.2 million had been received in grants, loans and donations,[15] the Trust was struggling to raise sufficient capital to tackle the huge backlog of repairs and maintenance of the building stock, for which it estimated it needed £25 million. It was also experiencing poor trading at some of its own commercial ventures such as the Crew's Quarters Club, and by 1990 was recording annual losses of £200,000. In this situation there was the real prospect of insolvency, and Sir Steuart concluded the only solution was to return to the government for a sizable additional capital sum, on the argument that the original endowment of £11.35 million was plainly insufficient, even on the basis of the specialist advice the government had received at the time.

What was thought to be an unanswerable case by the Trust was firmly rejected by the government of the day. The responsible minister in the DoE, David Trippier, replied in July 1990 that there was simply no prospect of a further endowment from the government. The Trust should essentially solve its own problems by recruiting additional trustees with the relevant experience to enable it to adopt a much more commercial approach to generating visitor and property income. From the department responsible for conservation also came the surprisingly gung-ho suggestion that the Trust might have to consider demolition of difficult-to-let buildings if it could not afford the refurbishment costs. The Trust was quite rightly aghast at this suggestion, pointing out that such examples were actually Scheduled Monuments and Listed Buildings. Not only was no more heard of this proposal, but the government soon took the opposite approach by agreeing in November 1990 to provide £1 million annually for three years through English Heritage.

Welcome though this was, it amounted to little more than sticking plaster. Losses continued, with a deficit budget of £500,000 being set for 1991/1992, but the DoE stuck to its view that there was no more big money available and that the Trust should reduce its expenditure to achieve economies rather than throw in the towel. Redundancies were therefore inevitable, coupled with all future plans for development of new galleries being placed in abeyance. The DoE did, however, agree to an independent review of the Trust's finances, carried out in early 1991 by Sir Francis Pemberton. This led to a second and then a third report, each one producing recommendations about the scale and timing of additional capital needed, which were unacceptable either to the Trust or DoE. Either way, no such further finance was offered.

Trustees and their advisors in 1995, Sir William Staveley (chairman) at centre.

[Chatham Historic Dockyard Trust]

Sir Steuart Pringle had retired as chairman[16] and was succeeded by Sir William Staveley. By 1995 the original endowment had dwindled to little over £1 million and the business was continuing to suffer operating losses. Around this time, the Trust then turned to Rochester-upon-Medway City Council, who offered essentially to take over the operation by providing £10 million of capital in exchange for occupying 6 of 10 places on a reconstituted board. While this was, not surprisingly, enthusiastically received by all the government interests – MoD, DoE, Department for National Heritage (DNH) and English Heritage – the attraction was less clear for the Trust, and this particular initiative eventually stalled. Instead, it stimulated a much more robust approach by the Trust to justifying the dockyard's future spending needs. Bruce Robertson, the then chief executive, prepared a fully researched capital development programme with the objective of increasing income from commercial and leisure activities over a ten-year period, costed at about £9 million at 1996 prices.

Fortunately for Chatham, at exactly that time the Conservative government under John Major established the National Lottery, with the prospect of substantial new resources likely to be available for heritage projects. Not surprisingly, therefore, Sir William Staveley urged the trustees to accept that Chatham Historic Dockyard should be one of the first applications made to the newly established Heritage Lottery Fund (HLF), and consultants KPMG were employed to provide a foundation for such an application.

HMS *Gannet* (1878) after her arrival in No. 3 Dock in 1987. [Chatham Historic Dockyard Trust]

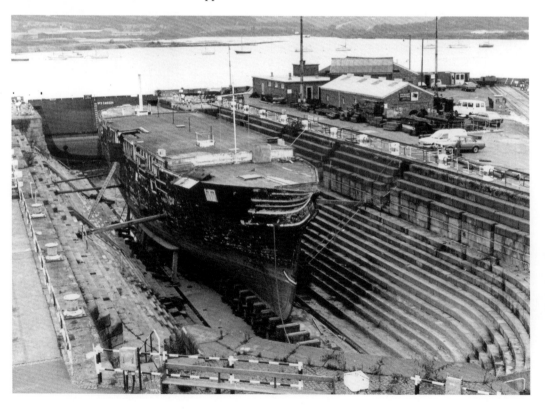

The KPMG work was much the most thorough and professionally presented analysis of all the many consultants' studies of the historic dockyard's opportunities and achievable outcomes. It stress-tested the Trust's latest capital development programme and not only endorsed its basic legitimacy, but took the courageous step of demonstrating it was not sufficiently ambitious if the finances were to be put on a long-term sustainable footing. KPMG therefore strongly recommended adding completion of the *Gannet* restoration programme as a key icon of the historic dockyard, coupled with a range of museum improvement and infrastructure works amounting to a revised total of £14.7 million. It also advised that the government should also provide some revenue funding on a continuing basis.

In turn, the KPMG recommendations formed the basis of a formal application to the HLF and a revised proposal to Rochester-upon-Medway City Council. In 1997, HLF approved a capital grant of £8.8 million, the city council contributed £4.8 million, and the balance up to the recommended £14.7 million came from English Heritage and other trusts. This enabled the whole project timetable to be reset, together with a wide range of contextual requirements such as a comprehensive conservation plan for the historic dockyard. In addition, KPMG had exhaustively scrutinised the historic dockyard's pricing policies, its identity, the requirements to radically improve the visitor environment, and the Trust's marketing and development capabilities to carry out these changes. Crucially, HLF provided a further £1.2 million in revenue support, and DNH (subsequently Department for Culture, Media and Sport, now Department for Digital, Culture, Media and Sport) agreed to grant aid of around £300,000 annually.

Collectively, this amounted to a revolution in the Trust's financial resources. At last the Trust was in the position to realistically carry out the property development programme and develop the visitor attractions to generate respectable income. In turn, this new-found confidence spawned valuable partnerships with other bodies, for example the Rochester Bridge Trust, who granted £2.5 million for the conversion of the Clocktower Building to become the University of Kent's Bridge Wardens' College.

Subsequently, other major HLF grants towards the Command of the Oceans and Fitted Rigging House projects means that the total investment from this source alone has been over £30 million. Together with many other grants towards specific projects from a range of other benefactors, the historic dockyard has benefited from external financial support on a scale unimaginable in 1984, and without which there is the certainty that the Trust would have found itself unable to continue.

The next major change took place in the late 1990s to implement the KPMG proposals. This saw a new chairman in Sir Nicholas Hunt following the death of Sir William Staveley in 1997, and a change of chief executive, with Bruce Robertson being succeeded by Joe Creighton in 1998. They embarked upon the range of improvements for which funding was now available – principally completion of the *Gannet* restoration, No. 7 Slip, and the Sail and Colour Loft – and in so doing helped lay the foundations for much of the Trust's recent success.

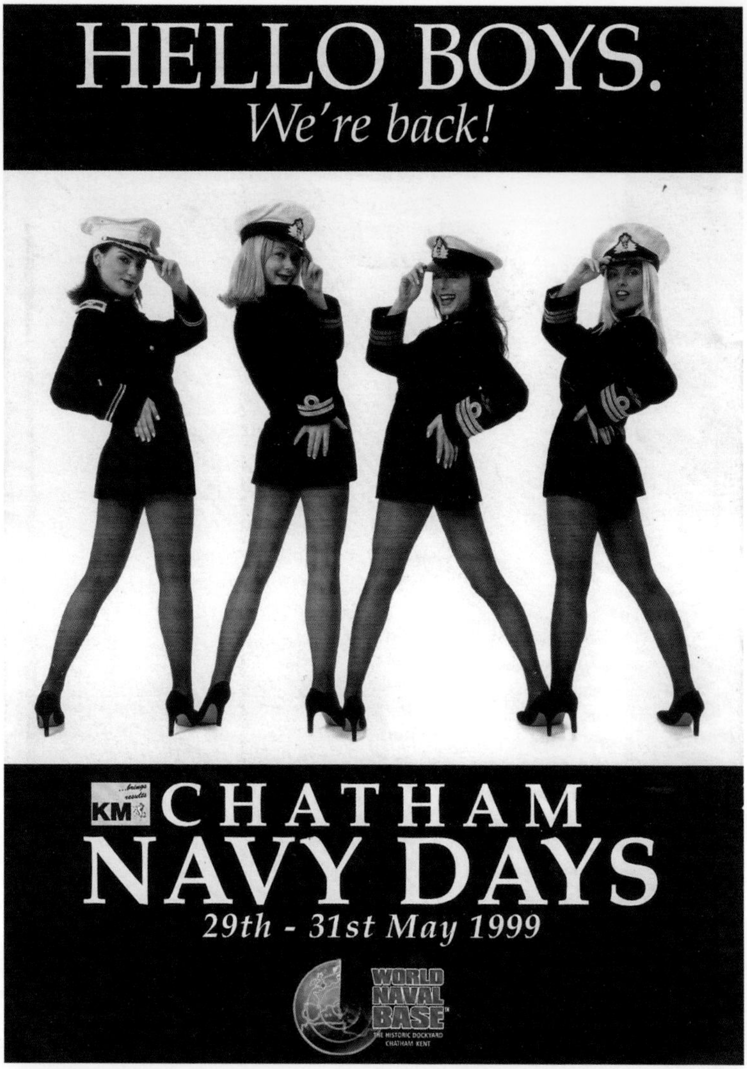

HELLO BOYS.
We're back!

KM CHATHAM
NAVY DAYS
29th - 31st May 1999

WORLD
NAVAL
BASE
THE HISTORIC DOCKYARD
CHATHAM KENT

World Naval Base era –
promotional material for the
return of Navy Days to Chatham.
[Chatham Historic Dockyard Trust]

However, they also took the view that Chatham Historic Dockyard should try the option touched on earlier in this chapter of becoming a much more overt and explicit mainstream tourist attraction, concentrating arguably less on the intrinsic conservation attributes of the place than using it as a backdrop for large visitor-attracting events. The criticism was levelled at whether these initiatives helped visitors understand the nature and purpose of the historic dockyard rather than simply chasing volume and income. The rebranding of Chatham Historic Dockyard as the World Naval Base, the reintroduction of Chatham Navy Days in 1999, and encouraging staff to dress up in replica naval uniform did not last, and was not a successful or happy chapter in the historic dockyard's recent history.

The most recent phase has been the return to a much more thoughtful and stable strategic approach to the development of the historic dockyard's assets, under the guidance of the long-standing chief executive Bill Ferris, chairman Sir Ian Garnett, and his recent successor Sir Trevor Soar. They have collectively put the Trust on a firm financial footing while maintaining and enhancing Chatham's role as the world's most complete Georgian naval dockyard. The major achievements have been bringing several of the difficult buildings such as the Smithery and Fitted Rigging House back into use, substantially improving visitor facilities through the Command of the Oceans project, establishing the University of Kent as one of the major users of dockyard buildings, and maintaining the operation of the historic Ropery as a commercial undertaking in what have been difficult trading circumstances.

Since its closure and renaissance, Chatham Historic Dockyard has become an exemplar in the field of large-scale conservation and regeneration of historic environments. The Trust was instrumental in establishing a network of like-minded historic dockyards around the world and hosted an inaugural conference in 1998 exploring the lessons to be applied to future projects.[17]

Reviewing the period since 1984, the contribution of several organisations and individuals stand out. Without the championing and financial support of Kent County Council at the outset, and latterly the former Rochester-upon-Medway City Council and HLF, the Trust would never had succeeded. Maintaining the integrity of the historic dockyard and everything it represents has largely fallen on the shoulders of Richard Holdsworth, appointed as curator in 1985 as one of the Trust's very first employees and still in post as director of heritage, public engagement and learning. John Spence was a trustee from day one until 2017, whose unprecedented record has been recognised by the Trust in making him a third statutory member, in the company of the two secretaries of state.

While challenges remain, such as how best to make the most of the Commissioners House and No. 3 Slip, and finding a satisfactory use for the interface land, the overriding conclusion must be that Chatham Historic Dockyard looks, feels and functions much better than at any time in the last 35 years. For that, the Trust can be genuinely proud of its achievements, and those who campaigned in the early 1980s so forcefully for its establishment can regard themselves as justifiably vindicated.

Notes

1   The Chatham naval base is defined as all the former Royal Navy operations at Chatham comprising the dockyard, the Royal Naval barracks at HMS *Pembroke* and the training establishment at HMS *Collingwood*.

2   Though in the event this was never achieved.

3   At the time an inspector of ancient monuments at English Heritage responsible for identifying the historic importance of buildings and engineering works in the Royal Navy's operational home bases.

4   The then director of the Ironbridge Gorge Museum Trust, later at the National Maritime Museum, Science Museum and chairman of English Heritage.

5   And which are now important elements of the Trust's galleries.

6   The case for a new Medway crossing was championed over the previous ten years, particularly by Michael Lewis, leader of Gillingham Borough Council at the time, and also fortuitously a member of the Rochester Bridge Trust. The Bridge Trust promoted the Medway Tunnel Act 1990 to obtain the powers to build the tunnel, which were subsequently delegated to Kent County Council. In addition,

the Trust contributed £5 million towards the £60 million cost of the scheme as well as purchasing all the necessary land. Most recently, the Trust gifted the tunnel to Medway Council rather than assume full responsibility for operating it in 2021 as originally envisaged. The link roads are the Wainscott Northern Bypass and the Gillingham Northern Link, constructed by Kent County Council at a cost of £95 million.

7   Even then, consultants were querying the appropriateness of the boundaries of the historic dockyard and why the land either side of the mast pond was excluded.

8   Also proposed was the demolition of buildings considered then to make little contribution, including the Police Section House, now in the ownership of Homes England and currently the subject of a proposed refurbishment by the Trust for use by the University of Kent.

9   Crucially, he was also a Kent MP (for Dover) and therefore personal relationships were already well established.

10   The chairman of English Estates at that time, which had taken over responsibility for the modern dockyard; this enabled a strong partnership between the two main components of the former dockyard to be established from the start.

11   Of which MoD provided £10 million and DoE £1.35 million.

12   For example, a paper in 1983 by John Goodspeed, the last civil secretary to the Port Admiral; Binney and Martin, *Alive or Mothballed* 1984; and a detailed Development Strategy prepared by Kent County Council in September 1984.

13   This was a concern which was to raise its head again in future negotiations on funding.

14   Sadly, neither enterprise survived on a commercial basis, and CHDT established its own company Master Ropemakers to take over the Ropery operation when Cosalt departed for Northern Ireland in 1987.

15   Of which Kent County Council (£600,000) and English Heritage (£500,000) were the largest providers.

16   In 1992.

17   RENDOC 1998.

References

Ancient Monuments Directorate, Department of the Environment 1981 *The Royal Dockyards*

Binney, M and Martin, K 1984 *Chatham Historic Dockyard Alive or Mothballed*. London: SAVE Britain's Heritage

Chatham Historic Dockyard Trust 1998 *RENDOC 98 Conference Proceedings*

Coad, Jonathan 1982 'Historic Architecture of Chatham Dockyard 1700–1850'. *Mariner's Mirror* **68**.2 (May), 133–85

Coad, Jonathan 1983 *Historic Architecture of the Royal Navy, An Introduction*. London: Victor Gollancz

Deakin, W H 1981 *Chatham Historic Dockyard: Planning Appraisal*. Kent County Council

Deakin, W H 1982 *Royal Naval Base Chatham Studies: 1 Planning Appraisal*. Kent County Council

Deakin, W H 1982 *Royal Naval Base Chatham Studies: 1a HMS* Pembroke *Planning Appraisal*. Kent County Council

Deakin, W H 1984 *Development Strategy for the Chatham Historic Dockyard*. Kent County Council

Deakin, W H, Fraser, I A and Williams, R S 1982 *Royal Naval Base Chatham Studies: 3 Conclusions and Recommendations*

Fraser, I A and Williams, R S 1982 *Royal Naval Base Chatham Studies: 2 Medway Urban Area Study*

Frederick Gibberd Coombes and Partners 1985 *Chatham Maritime and Chatham Historic Dockyard Development Plan*

Gillingham Borough Council and Rochester-upon-Medway City Council 1987 *Chatham Maritime and Chatham Historic Dockyard Development Brief*

Goodspeed, John 1983 *Chatham Historic Dockyard – Some Project Ideas for a Future Manager*

KPMG, 1996 *Chatham Historic Dockyard Development Strategy*

MacDougall, Philip 1981 *The Chatham Dockyard Story*. Rochester: Rochester Press

MacDougall, Philip 1994 *Chatham Dockyard in Old Photographs*. Stroud: Sutton Publishing Ltd

Richard Ellis Venture Consultants Ltd 1989 *The Chatham Historic Dockyard, Progress since 1982 and the Future Potential*

Rochester-upon-Medway City Council 1986 *Chatham Historic Dockyard Development and Design Brief*

US Department of the Interior 1995 *Charlestown Navy Yard Boston*, National Historical Park Handbook

Wilson, Hugh and Womersley, Lewis/Ellis, Richard 1982 *Chatham Historic Dockyard Study on Economic and Environmental Opportunities*

View across Museum Square, the site of No. 2 Smithery demolished in 1981 before dockyard closure, towards HMS *Gannet* (1878), showing the outcome of the successive programme of repair and restoration works, many funded with the support of the National Lottery Heritage Fund. [CHDT/VHH/James Brittain]

5 Preservation through reuse

Paul Jardine

Introduction

I was appointed by the Heritage Lottery Fund (now the National Lottery Heritage Fund) in 1999 to be the lead monitor on all current Heritage Fund-supported projects at Chatham Historic Dockyard. This became a five-year assignment involving over 15 discrete projects, some £15 million of investment by the National Lottery Heritage Fund (with some of this funding coming from the National Heritage Memorial Fund) and the most complex and enthralling project that I have ever had the opportunity to monitor.

Until 1999 I had not visited Chatham Historic Dockyard but was aware of its role during the Falklands War and as a developing visitor attraction from 1984. During the 1980s and 1990s, if you lived outside Kent and the South East of England you would have required a keen interest in heritage and visitor attractions to be aware of Chatham Historic Dockyard's emerging new role.

The transformation of Chatham Historic Dockyard between 1999 and 2020 has occurred during a period of exceptional change in consumer motivations and behaviours. The way consumers act, communicate and record their experiences has changed, and the growth of online communities has redefined how relationships are maintained and curated.

The transformation of Chatham Historic Dockyard has redefined how historic sites can preserve heritage assets and make them relevant to contemporary audiences for the purposes of living (as homes), working (as offices and workshops), learning (as formal and informal places of education) and visiting (as a leisure attraction).

Chatham Historic Dockyard Trust

Established in 1984, Chatham Historic Dockyard Trust (CHDT/the Trust) identified its primary objectives as 'the preservation of The Historic Dockyard Chatham, the most complete 18th Century dockyard in the world, and the education of the public in its historical, architectural and archaeological importance'. The specific charitable objectives are as follows:

1. To secure for the public benefit the preservation and use of the historic dockyard at Chatham in the County of Kent in a manner appropriate to its archaeological, historical and architectural importance.

2. To promote and foster for the public benefit a wide knowledge and understanding of the archaeological, historical and architectural significance of the historic dockyard.

These charitable objectives are achieved through the following strategic objectives:

- To maintain excellence in the sympathetic preservation and use of the historic dockyard, its buildings, ships and collections.

- To engage the widest possible audience in learning about the significant role of the former Royal dockyard at Chatham and its people in supporting the Royal Navy from sail to steam and nuclear power over a 400-year period.
- To provide an unmatched, inspirational and enjoyable experience for all users of the historic dockyard – whether visitors, tenants, residents or students – that exceeds their expectations.

The early years

From 1984 to 1996 the dockyard attracted an average of 72,500 visits per annum. Admittedly, the visit number was higher at the end of this period of operation than at the beginning, with the annual number of visits around 100,000. This initial period of operation from 1984 saw the development of the visitor experience and some commercial developments. By 1996, an initial grant of £11 million had been eroded, with only £1 million remaining. With significant operating deficits, both accumulated and anticipated, the future operation of the dockyard required increased income from both visitors and commercial property. This is the context in which KPMG was commissioned in 1996 to produce a Development Strategy for the dockyard.

Development Strategy

The Development Strategy considered the scope for growing the number of visits, the associated admission income, secondary visitor expenditure, and commercial property income.

The Development Strategy identified an opportunity to develop the annual number of visits to 150,000. This represented a 50 per cent increase on the then current performance and a 100 per cent increase on the long-term average achieved to that point. Estimating visit numbers is both difficult and fraught with complications.

In the 20-year period from 1999 to 2018 the dockyard attracted an average of 144,000 visits per annum. This was supported by an events programme throughout, and the core visitor attraction achieved over 163,000 visits in 2018/19 (excluding the additional 28,000 event visitors).

The importance of obtaining a realistic and achievable projection of visit numbers has several benefits beyond securing an estimate of potential admission income. The visit volume and the associated seasonal pattern of visitation allows an accurate assessment of the peak day and typical day-visit volume and the scaling of facilities to deliver a quality visitor experience. Visitor feedback reflected in the 1996 Development Strategy highlighted the limited refreshment and toilet facilities. While too few toilets is an issue for visitor satisfaction, too many is an operational cost that is not required. Similarly, the extent of an attraction required to provide up to 150,000 visitors with an enjoyable experience does not mean that every historic building or asset be accessible to visitors. As with single historic properties with many rooms, the visitor experience can be created and curated in a fraction of the 100 buildings that are present in the dockyard.

The Development Strategy recognised the need for iconic experiences. It both identified and prioritised these and included HMS

Aerial view showing the site's dry docks following the 1998–2004 NLHF-funded development programme. The Trust's three historic warships are clearly visible. Left to right: HMS *Gannet* 1878, HM Submarine *Ocelot* 1962 and HMS *Cavalier* 1944.
[Chatham Historic Dockyard Trust]

Gannet and Museum Square Landscaping. These were supplemented with a series of other visitor experience projects, including HMS *Cavalier*. These addressed the acknowledged weaknesses of the pre-1996 visitor experience, provided iconic experiences not replicable elsewhere in Kent or the South East, and improved the quality of the public realm on site for the benefit of visitors, residents and businesses. While the enhancements to the visitor experience were essential to the development of Chatham from its position in 1996, these were measured, and addressed the identified visitor market opportunity. This avoided the temptation to do more than was necessary.

Masterplans and development strategies need to balance need and opportunity. Several masterplans have failed to be delivered or, if delivered, have failed to achieve the outcomes, or could have achieved their outcomes more efficiently.

Chatham Dockyard had an immense need to repair and consolidate the important buildings on site, but avoided the assumption that these should all have a direct role in the visitor experience. Instead, the Development Strategy recognised that the visitors needed iconic experiences, a site that was well presented and explained, and an understanding of both the site's history and the development strategy of mixed use.

The Development Strategy was instrumental in confirming and specifying the role of commercial property based on detailed analysis of the property market. The commercial property strategy identified a range of uses including offices, light industrial, storage, vehicle parking, education, residential lettings, and moorings that would provide the necessary diversification and development potential across the site in a manner that would complement and balance the visitor attraction operations.

The total property income from rents and service charges in 1996 was some £572,000. These grew to £2.44 million in 2018. This represents a growth of 228 per cent over 23 years, or 5.55 per cent per annum. The Development Strategy projected growth in commercial property income over an initial ten-year period of 6.3 per cent per annum. The achieved growth has been dependent on several factors, not least the preservation of buildings and their availability to the market.

Chatham Historic Dockyard as a visitor attraction

Chatham Historic Dockyard has provided visitor access since 1984. However, the comparison in the visitor experience between 1999 and 2019 demonstrates the transformation in terms of variety, scale, quality and accessibility. The 1996 Development Strategy highlights the 'site's great historic and architectural importance'. The term authenticity is not used in the Development Strategy, but that is implied and is the term that has become increasingly used to identify the experiences that today's visitors are seeking from heritage and other visitor attractions.

The Development Strategy examined the use of the Trust's historic assets and recognised that the dockyard's strengths and weaknesses were as follows:

Strengths
- The Dockyard is real history and there is plenty to see and many stories to tell;
- There is an established visitor base and it is widely recognised as the main attraction in North Kent and important in tourism terms at the sub-regional level.

Weaknesses
- It lacks a clear identity and an icon attraction/experience; many visitors do not have a clear idea of what they will experience;
- Once at the site, there is a lack of adequate orientation to enable the visitor to put different elements of the site in context. The exhibitions are educational but lack appeal to a wider audience, especially children and families; and
- The site is very large, relatively unattractive and has no internal transport. There are limited refreshment and toilet facilities.

The strengths identified have been developed and added to in the period since 1996 and the weaknesses have been systematically addressed. Some of the weaknesses proved difficult to address and have required several attempts to address them.

Chatham Historic Dockyard as a landlord

Preservation through reuse has been a key part of the redevelopment strategy and has been instrumental in balancing the uses of the dockyard buildings, attracting users in terms of employers and employees and residents.

A key user group at the dockyard has been the University of Kent. It took over its first building in 2006, the Clocktower Building, and has subsequently developed its presence and expanded its estate. Chatham is now home to the university's Centre of Music and Audio Technology and, most recently, the Medway arm of the Kent Business School in the Sail and Colour Loft, with a 300-seat lecture theatre in the Royal Dockyard Church. The Galvanising Shop houses the university's café.

The dockyard is also home to smaller enterprises, and many of these are in the creative sector. The Joiners' Shop provides accommodation for some 40 small creative businesses. While commercial property was an integral component of the Development Strategy, the delivery of it required an approach that was both entrepreneurial and dynamic, creating opportunities rather than waiting for them.

The Dockyard also has 115 homes and the approximately 400 residents provide a valuable addition to the mix of interests and uses of the historic buildings.

The Heritage Lottery Fund (now the National Lottery Heritage Fund)

The Heritage Fund's involvement in the dockyard has been long running, extensive and wide reaching. It is also true to state that the relationship between the parties has not always been easy. Lessons have been learned on all sides. These are considered briefly below.

The Heritage Fund has developed its role in the UK heritage sector over several strategic plans and more recently through its strategic frameworks. The early engagement by the Heritage Fund with the Trust and the dockyard recognised the significance of the heritage assets and the need to provide financial support to achieve the transition to a sustainable heritage site. The Heritage Fund's first grant award was made in 1996.

The awarding of the Heritage Fund grant in 1996 was enabled by the Secretary of State for National Heritage, Virginia Bottomley, who committed in December 1996 to providing an annual revenue grant of up to £300,000 from 1998/99. The commitment of this revenue grant was

The Joiners' Shop – Centre for Creative Business.
[Chatham Historic Dockyard Trust]

The Joiners' Shop – interior view of the first floor of the Joiners' Shop, one of the Trust's first major interventions to adapt buildings for reuse by introducing 'buildings within buildings', enabling modern facilities to be provided in a way that accentuates historic fabric and structure.
[Chatham Historic Dockyard Trust/ Nebulo Strata]

supported by the KPMG report that reviewed the Trust's ten-year plan and considered how sustainability could be achieved.

The initial Heritage Fund grant support was £10 million and was awarded to address a range of projects grouped under a variety of purposes. This was combined with a significant grant of £4.7 million from Medway Council and £0.5 million from English Heritage. This initial Heritage Fund grant was subsequently increased by £2.5 million to address the needs of HMS *Gannet* and the building repair and adaptation programme. Additional funding of £1 million was also secured through the European Regional Development Fund's Interreg II (1994–9) programme.

Specific visitor attraction projects, including HMS *Gannet* and HMS *Cavalier*, were subsequently added. A significant proportion of the projects were described as site infrastructure and included renewal of the electrical distribution network; repair of the river wall and tidal flaps; essential repairs and redecoration to scheduled ancient monuments; and dockyard infrastructure renewal. Several buildings were identified for a range of support from preparatory design works to repair and renewals, e.g., the Joiners' Shop and No. 1 Smithery. This flexibility over the application of grant funds was crucial in identifying a way forward for the overall site and in resolving issues facing individual buildings. Finally, there was revenue support designed to alleviate some of the operating deficit by contributing to key operating costs, e.g. insurance.

HMS *Gannet* (1878) against the backdrop of restored covered slipways.
[Chatham Historic Dockyard Trust]

HMS *Gannet* (1878): Removal of the poop deck planking revealed the extent of corrosion – largely the result of the Navy's use of mahogany rather than teak in this area of the ship at her 1886 refit. [Chatham Historic Dockyard Trust]

HMS *Gannet* (1878): The new rivetted poop deck takes shape. [Chatham Historic Dockyard Trust]

HMS *Cavalier* afloat in No. 2 Dock in 2016. Both *Cavalier* and *Gannet* are kept afloat in dry docks specially modified to keep water in. Doing so helps fully support their hulls.
[Chatham Historic Dockyard Trust]

HMS *Cavalier* is preserved at Chatham as the National Destroyer Memorial. The associated monument, a bas relief sculpture by Kenneth Potts, was unveiled by HRH Prince Philip on 14 November 2007. Admiral Sir Ian Garnett, chairman of the Trust watches on.
[Chatham Historic Dockyard Trust]

The initial relationship between the Trust and the Heritage Fund was difficult. In part this was due to a misunderstanding that the Heritage Fund would act like some other funders and provide the funds with little involvement. The Heritage Fund's desire to ensure that its funding achieved the desired outcomes meant that it was more involved than other funders and more involved than the Trust was used to and had expected.

Following the unveiling of the memorial, HRH Prince Philip toured the ship, meeting the volunteers who helped restore her as well as veterans who had served on board destroyers during the Second World War and after. Here in the wardroom he is seen with Richard Holdsworth, director of heritage, public engagement and learning and Mick Keir, volunteer and chairman of the Friends of HMS *Cavalier* Trust.
[Chatham Historic Dockyard Trust]

The Heritage Fund had a desire to be flexible, but this required a detailed understanding of the initial project proposals, the progress on the project proposals, and the need and opportunity to enhance these by redirecting the expenditure to a revised specification or revised project. In 1999/2000 the Trust was required to modify the project proposal previously agreed with the Heritage Fund as a consequence of the following factors:

- The impact of inflation on the original budgeted costs
- The impact of emergent works
- Delays to the capital programme

The Heritage Fund's decision to provide the support and flexibility was critical to the transformation of the dockyard. However, this was matched in importance by key management and governance changes. The arrival of Bill Ferris as chief executive of CHDT changed the manner of operation. Relationships with external stakeholders were regarded as valuable rather than with suspicion. There was explicit recognition that funders, not limited to the Heritage Fund, had a legitimate interest in understanding what was being done, why it was being done, and how it was being done.

The new management and governance from 2000 more clearly demonstrated an understanding of the imperative for change, the scale of change required, and the pace of change. The path for completion of the series of Heritage Fund-supported projects become clearer, decision-making better informed, and mistakes identified and rectified. This provided confidence to funders and marked a change to what had previously become an increasingly fractious relationship.

Subsequent Heritage Fund grants were awarded for

- No. 1 Smithery, £5 million Heritage grant
- Command of the Oceans, £4.5 million Heritage grant
- Fitted Rigging House, £4.8 million Heritage Enterprise grant

Financial performance

The various successes of Chatham Historic Dockyard do not mask the financial challenges of operating a heritage-based visitor attraction. Across the UK, heritage attractions require and receive significant financial support from philanthropic sources, trusts and foundations, local authorities, and government departments and agencies. Some are fortunate to have access to endowment funds. Some achieve financial independence because of favourable operating conditions and some luck. Those that achieve financial independence are in a minority. Unlike commercial leisure operations, heritage attractions have some heavy burdens in terms of management and maintenance and are faced with constraints on what the visitor market collectively and individually is prepared to pay for admission.

While the Premier League can charge £30 for a 90-minute football match and Legoland Windsor Resort can charge £60 for a day ticket, these charges are not achievable for heritage attractions in the UK. UK consumers assess the Premier League and Legoland Windsor as providing value for money. Stonehenge charges £21.10 for an adult, without gift aid, and the Churchill War Rooms charges £22 for a 'standard' adult admission (2020 prices). However, should these and other heritage attractions try to charge higher levels of admission, the consumers' value-for-money assessment would mean a dramatic reduction in visitor numbers, admission income and secondary income. It is not surprising that heritage attractions require revenue support.

The scale of the financial achievements at Chatham Historic Dockyard can be measured by comparing the 1996 Development Strategy and the 2018 financial statements. Visitor admission income had achieved a level some 3.6 times the 1996 level. Property income had achieved a level some 3.3 times the 1996 level. The Development Strategy projected an increase in property income of 73 per cent and an increase in visitor income of 20 per cent. Property income remained greater in absolute terms, but visitor income achieved a growth rate considerably higher than expected. However, the visitor operations reported a considerable operating deficit, reflecting the property, equipment and staffing costs. Property operations excluding development projects achieved a surplus of income over expenditure. This position has been achieved recently and in part due to the significant contribution provided by the Fitted Rigging House and its letting income and performance. It produces £486,000 per annum from 9,500 sq m (including some non-commercial space) funded through an NLHF Heritage Enterprise grant of £4.8 million and £32 million of match funding.

Chatham Dockyard has achieved its financial performance despite having to trade through the 2008 recession and enduring a significant period of austerity.

Chatham Dockyard has taken advantage of a range of support and beneficial tax treatment available to UK charities. The gift-aid scheme operated by the Treasury has allowed the Trust to recover gift aid on qualifying admissions, where UK taxpayers have elected to gift aid their admission. This was a significant source of income for the Trust in 2018/19. The gift aid uptake percentage is approximately 70 per cent of individual visitors in recent years.

The Trust receives 80 per cent business rates relief due to its charitable status. Until the end of March 2017, the Trust also received an additional 20 per cent discretionary business rates relief from Medway Council. This was removed from 1 April 2017, which means that the Trust now pays 20 per cent business rates on all those buildings occupied by the Trust for the museum element of its operations. All buildings occupied by commercial tenants attract business rates at the full rate to the occupier.

The introduction of the museum and galleries exhibition tax relief in 2017 has allowed the Trust to claim a financial benefit for qualifying expenditure on exhibitions which were not separately charged or grant funded. The Trust made its first claim for 2017/18 and has continued to do so.

Lessons learned

There are several lessons to be learned from the experience of CHDT. These include the following:

Development Strategy/masterplan

The achievement of the Trust owes much to the Development Strategy prepared in 1996 by KPMG. It provides an exemplar in both what it includes and what is excluded. It deliberately did not try to resolve every issue facing the dockyard but provided clarity on the critical issues and what needed to be done next to address these.

The KPMG report explicitly considered and rejected the option 'to abandon its museum and visitor attraction objectives and focus all attention on letting property'. This option was rejected on the basis that the move to being only a property company would remove opportunities to secure grant assistance for the heritage assets. This appreciation of the 'heritage deficit' in the management and development of heritage assets resulted in the most appropriate option for the long-term survival and sustainability of Chatham Dockyard.

The KPMG Development Strategy provided clarity over the proposed direction of travel for the Trust across its key areas of activity: property development, visitor experience, and development projects. The property market analysis and visitor market analysis contained in the Development Strategy are central to the understanding of the conclusions and recommendations.

Development Strategy as a roadmap not a blueprint

A critical aspect of the transformation of the dockyard was the recognition by the Trust and their consultants that the Development Strategy was a roadmap and not a blueprint. The Development Strategy did not identify every project that the dockyard would need to implement. It did not provide a specification for each identified project and did not provide detailed annual budgets for the operation of the dockyard. It did, however, identify the critical projects that needed to be developed and implemented to deliver further progress towards the completion of the transformation of the dockyard into a leading visitor attraction. The financial information provided estimates and projections that reflected orders of magnitude rather than highly detailed and precise figures and targets. It also made clear that capital grant income was critical to the Trust's success.

No. I Smithery in c 1999. This semi-derelict building at the heart of the historic dockyard by then had become one of the Trust's most intractable problems.
[Chatham Historic Dockyard Trust]

No. I Smithery – interior view of what would become the 2010 building's new Orientation Gallery – Before.
[Chatham Historic Dockyard Trust /Slater Crosby]

No. 1 Smithery: 2010 Orientation
Gallery – After.
[CHDT/VHH/James Brittain]

No. 1 Smithery: External view 2010.
[CHDT/VHH/James Brittain]

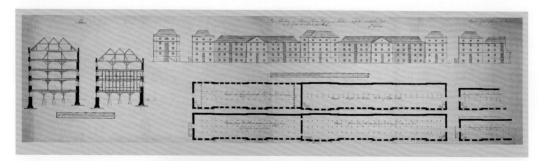

Plan for the Anchor Wharf Fitted Rigging House and Storehouse No. 3. The Trust's last large underutilised building was adapted to provide office, gallery and archive storage. Fully let shortly after opening in 2018, an economic impact study for the historic dockyard by DC Research calculated that by then the site's local economic impact was c £30 million per annum.
[The National Archives]

Fitted Rigging House – new central cores by Baynes & Mitchell Architects provides stair and lift access to all floors.
[Chatham Historic Dockyard Trust]

Fitted Rigging House: New stud partition walls provide fire separation to both the new offices and central core – installed in a way to highlight the building's historic fabric and structure.
[Chatham Historic Dockyard Trust]

The Fitted Rigging House was opened on 18 October 2018 by the Minister for Arts, Heritage and Tourism, Michael Ellis MP, shown here on a tour of the building with Sir Trevor Soar (left) and Bill Ferris, chief executive 2001–20 (right).
[Chatham Historic Dockyard Trust/Paul Herron]

Constant challenge

The Development Strategy provided the Trust with opportunities to adapt to changing circumstances and to recognise where improvements could be made. A feature of Chatham Historic Dockyard has been the ability to recognise where addressing key buildings is a priority and when to reconsider previous investments that could be improved. Specific examples over the past 20 years must include No. 1 Smithery, a partnership with the Imperial War Museum and National Maritime Museum. This award-winning £13 million (including £5 million from NLHF) project has taken a significant derelict building complex and repurposed it as collections storage and exhibition galleries.

The Fitted Rigging House perhaps exemplifies the Trust's approach to development and reuse. An initial project at the Fitted Rigging House in the early 2000s was to restore the external elevations, first floor and the ground, with the latter used for the Museum of the Dockyard. In 2018 the renovation was finally completed, with the upper floors being prepared as space for commercial tenancies. This mix of use follows the principles established in the 1996 Development Strategy and delivers a project that is entirely consistent with the outcome envisaged more than 20 years earlier.

The final example that demonstrates the Trust's approach to the site's development and the careful balance between opportunities and needs is the redevelopment of the visitor entrance with café and exhibition galleries. This project was, like others, in gestation from 1995. 1995 saw the discovery of the frame of the 18th-century warship the *Namur* under the Mast Houses. The final redevelopment of this part of the site, undertaken by Baynes & Mitchell Architects in 2017, cleverly resolved

The 'ship beneath the floor' archaeological find of ships' timbers beneath the Wheelwrights' Shop in 1995 brought attempts to bring the building back into reuse to a halt for 20 years, but led to Command of the Oceans – a finalist in the 2017 RIBA Stirling Prize.
[Chatham Historic Dockyard Trust]

Command of the Oceans – opened by Admiral of the Fleet the Lord Boyce in May 2016, Left to right: Vice Admiral Jerry Kidd, Fleet Commander, Admiral Sir Ian Garnett, immediate past Trust chairman and his successor Sir Trevor Soar, the Lord Boyce.
[Chatham Historic Dockyard Trust/ Rikard Osterlund]

Command of the Oceans: External view of the new visitor entrance structure and ramp inserted between the Wheelwrights' Shop and the Mast Houses and Mould Loft to the design of Baynes & Mitchell Architects.
[Chatham Historic Dockyard Trust/ Rikard Osterlund]

Command of the Oceans: New floor in the Wheelwrights' Shop, inserted over the Ship's Timbers viewing gallery, to provide accommodation for the Discovery Centre, and the site's ticketing and retail shop.
[Chatham Historic Dockyard Trust/ Rikard Osterlund]

a number of physical, operational and logistical conundrums, while enhancing the visitor experience by incorporating visitor access to the site, the historic timbers, the visitor café and the exhibitions in the Mast Houses.

Financial sustainability

The existence of a development strategy or masterplan is a necessary but not sufficient condition for achieving redevelopment. Too many masterplans assume that a sustainable outcome will be achieved. Chatham Historic Dockyard Trust's development strategy was truthful in identifying that financial sustainability would require earned income from property and from visitors, and unearned income in the form of long-term grant support, in this case from the Department for Digital, Culture, Media and Sport. The instrumental report from KPMG in 1996 built a detailed case based on a property review and a visitor market assessment. Crucially, it did not assume financial sustainability would be an outcome. In fact, both the base case and best case demonstrated the need for long-term revenue grant support.

The Trust has always recognised that the Development Strategy does not replace the need for a business plan or an annual budget. Business plans to accompany the 1996 Development Strategy were prepared in 1999 and in 2001 and subject to external scrutiny from the Heritage Fund.

Visitor experience

It is more clearly evidenced and acknowledged now than in 1999 and earlier that visitors value authentic experiences. Chatham Historic Dockyard has, with Heritage Fund investment, ensured the conservation and preservation of those assets that deliver authenticity. This includes not the mere act of conserving the heritage but doing so in a manner which contributes to the authenticity. A strong example of this was the agreement to repair HMS *Gannet* using traditional riveting techniques,

Admiral Sir Nicholas Hunt
(chairman 1998–2005) on the
twentieth anniversary of the Trust
in 2004.

[Chatham Historic Dockyard Trust]

despite the attendant noise, cost, disruption and the existence of cheaper alternatives. We each owe a debt of gratitude to my associate monitor and naval architect MRC (Tim) Parr for his expert guidance and commitment to the cause on this and other repair methodologies.

Leadership

Having been involved during a time at Chatham Historic Dockyard which saw considerable change in personnel in key board and executive positions, it is clear to me that the Trust has benefited hugely from the quality of governance and management and that has been amplified by the continuity of service provided by key members of the team. It is particularly noticeable that there is an appropriate and strong differentiation between board governance responsibilities and executive management functions. This is not always the case in heritage organisations, often to their detriment.

The core executive team, which has remained unchanged since 2000, includes Bill Ferris OBE DL (chief executive), Richard Holdsworth MBE (director of heritage public engagement and learning) and Chris Knott (chief financial officer until 2019).

In terms of trustees, Sir Nicholas Hunt GCB LVO DL provided an invaluable contribution from 1998 to 2005, a critical phase in the development of the dockyard and the Trust. He and his successors as chairman, Sir Ian Garnett KCB and Sir Trevor Soar KCB OBE, were instrumental in developing and maintaining relationships with key stakeholders, including the Heritage Fund, DCMS, local authorities and other stakeholders such as SEEDA. This relationship benefited from the significant interest shown by Sue Palmer, a Heritage Lottery Fund trustee, who continued this interest by becoming a trustee at CHDT from 2004 to 2013.

Organisational development

The continuity of employment should not and does not imply a static organisation. All organisations considering committing to a development strategy or masterplan must recognise that their organisation will have to develop if the impact of the development strategy or masterplan is to be realised, maintained and maximised. The Trust, like many museums and galleries implementing such strategies and plans, has undergone considerable organisational development. The recognition within the executive team and board of the essential skills required has led to considerable training and recruitment to ensure that the organisation remains fit for purpose. The Development Strategy identified some of the implications for the management team, but considerably more change has been implemented and required than identified in 1996. The Trust has a talent development and management strategy that continues this process of organisational development.

Project management

The governance and management team have also been assisted with additional resources. These have allowed the introduction of specialist project management expertise. The use of appropriate project managers to manage the external and internal resources of the project ensures that the management of the day-to-day operations is not jeopardised. At the dockyard, the executive team remained in control of each project, with all variations to agreed contracts being approved by the chief executive officer. The appointment of project managers also recognised the benefits of obtaining those with the requisite skills and capacity to manage the detail and complexity of project delivery. They were also selected for their experience of historic buildings and museum and gallery projects for managing both the external consultants and contractors and similarly for the appointment of project managers to co-ordinate the in-house and partner resources essential for project development and delivery.

This avoided the executive team becoming overloaded by attempting to provide the strategic planning, operational management and development, and the detailed day-to-day role in the delivery of major development projects.

Conclusions

Chatham Historic Dockyard has never lost its ambition. This has allowed it to progress one of the most significant transformation projects undertaken in the UK heritage sector in the past 35 years. The obvious projects include the restoration of the ships and other components of the visitor experience. The property projects include the range of working and learning facilities that have been developed and enjoyed by employers, employees and students. The hidden projects represent those that have consumed huge resources but allow the site to operate safely with resilience, and service and benefit all who have a responsibility and interest in the future of the dockyard.

The Development Strategy explicitly recognised the need for a mixed economy at the dockyard, both in the sense of earned income from leisure and property and from unearned income, the latter represented by the continued revenue support from the Department for Digital, Culture, Media and Sport and grant funding from a variety of sources including the Heritage Fund, government departments and agencies, trusts and foundations, and philanthropic sources. However, the existence of the Development Strategy does not mean that it will be implemented, will be successful, or sustainable in the long term.

The success in delivering the strategy reflects the combined effort of the trustees and the executive team, and the partnerships with a variety of stakeholders. These include tenants, funders and organisations with a keen interest in the future of Chatham Historic Dockyard as a means of preserving its past. The years since 1999 have been an extraordinary period of sustained delivery and achievement. The quality of the built environment at the dockyard has been transformed and the range of users and uses provides a vitality and vibrancy that is infectious. The Trust is well placed to continue this period of achievement into the future with the legacy of the efforts and outputs since 1984.

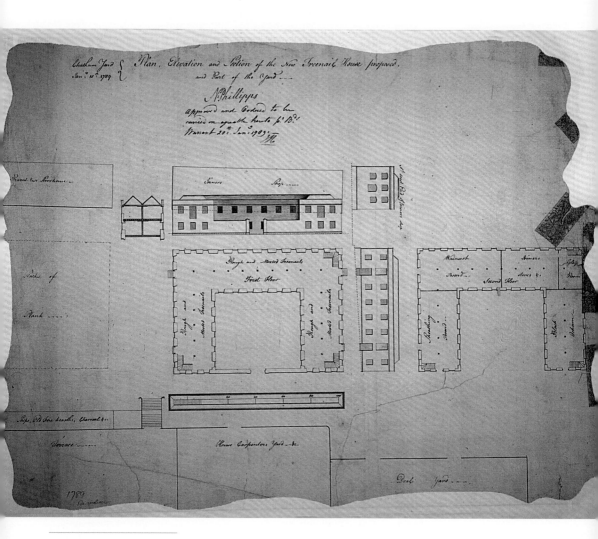

Joiners' Shop: 1789 plan
and elevation.
[The National Archives]

6 Policy into practice

Richard Holdsworth

During the Chatham Historic Dockyard Trust's first 15 years, its adaptation of buildings for new uses was generally based around simple refurbishments to bring spaces back into revenue-generating activity. Redecoration, renewal of services, particularly electrical supplies, and minimum alterations to internal structures were the norm, generally being all that could be afforded and, indeed, delivered, under contemporary thinking around the preservation, repair and adaptation of Scheduled Monuments and Listed Buildings. Examples of this approach can still be seen in buildings such as the House Carpenters' Shop and Admiral's Offices, where original internal compartmentalisation remained fit for modern uses as craft workshops, artists' workplaces and offices.

The 1998–2004 Heritage Lottery Fund development programme, based on the recommendations of the KPMG study (*see* Chapter 5), laid the foundations for tackling more difficult buildings, not the least through the wholesale renewal of the historic dockyard's high- and low-voltage cables and transformer stations which allowed for the reconnection of many more buildings and structures across the site. Since then the Trust has moved on from the 'simple' adaptations that went before to more complex interventions and adaptations in more sensitive historic buildings and structures. With the support of English Heritage (now Historic England) inspectors of ancient monuments (initially Jonathan Coad and then Peter Kendall), key funders and innovative architects, the Trust has played a major role in developing thinking about what was possible within such structures – and in many ways pushed the boundaries of previous thinking with significant and beneficial results.

The following four projects serve to demonstrate development of thinking and practice through the period from 2004 onwards and will be considered in some depth. Interlinked in nature, in some cases overlapping in development time, they also illustrate the diverse nature of reuse on site and its contribution to the wider development of the Medway and North Kent economy and sense of place. The approach to all is underpinned by three key conservation principles:

- Limiting loss of historic fabric
- Undertaking 'honest' repairs that remain visible to future generations
- Ensuring reversibility wherever possible

The Joiners' Shop: Adaptation to deliver a creative industries starter unit for Medway built to BREEAM standards for sustainable buildings

Located at the centre of the historic dockyard, the Joiners' Shop (scheduled monument and Grade II* listed) is a two-storey brick structure originally built in *c* 1789 as a treenail house (treenails were wooden 'nails' or pegs used in wooden ship construction). Originally constructed as a U-shaped building around a central open courtyard, it was rebuilt in 1854 as the yard's Joiners' Shop, with an enclosed courtyard and with new steam-powered woodworking machines including a saw and mortising and tenoning machines.

In 1984 the building was an empty shell, but one that provided clear evidence of its former uses, particularly with the remains of line-shafting routes and elements of fireproof construction including cast iron doors and windows.

Soon after the Trust took over the dockyard the Joiners' Shop became the home for a Manpower Services Commission (MSC)-funded ordnance project – identifying and recovering naval muzzle-loading guns from the wider dockyard site where they had been used as bollards. This later became a gallery space for the display of that collection until relocated in 2002 to the Museum of the Royal Dockyard in the Fitted Rigging House. The upper floor provided a base for the North Kent Architecture Centre (initially a joint venture between the Trust, Kent County Council and City

Joiners' Shop: Interior view of the ground floor showing the fireproof construction.

[Chatham Historic Dockyard Trust]

of Rochester Council) which has now developed into Design South East, an independent charity delivering built-environment design support across the South East of England and beyond.

Relocation of the Ordnance Collection and Architecture Centre to other spaces within the historic dockyard led to the space becoming empty and available for income-generating reuse. The Trust's building conservation statement of the time (part of the site's Conservation Management Plan, now in its fifth iteration) described the building thus:

> A building of **considerable significance**, the Joiners Shop provided accommodation for the dockyard's joiners, effectively from the introduction of mechanised woodworking processes in the mid-1850s until the closure of the dockyard in 1984. The building's earlier form as the Treenail House provides close links with the Dockyard of the Age of Sail and the ship construction process. Like many of the yard's buildings it received a new lease of life as a result of the introduction of new working practices, tools and equipment during the mechanisation of dockyard trades in the mid-nineteenth century and therefore can be regarded as forming part of two unique assemblages of buildings that have survived at Chatham – buildings and structures closely related to the construction of warships of the age of sail – and buildings and structures closely identified with the mechanisation of the dockyard during the nineteenth century and the introduction of new materials and technologies.

The statement identified three specific policies which were to guide development of a long-term sustainable future for the building:

1. The Joiners shop is presently empty and not in use. A new and sustainable use needs to be found for this structure during the period of this plan.
2. Although identified as a building of considerable importance, this significance is held in the structure of the building – not in its contents as very little remains of internal fixtures and fittings.
3. Key features of the building – particularly the cast iron floor beams to the upper floors, the 'fireproof' construction of the engine house, evidence for the installation of line shafting and the elegant long thin ribbon metal window on the first floor eastern elevation, should be protected in any adaptation for reuse. Original 'office' accommodation and early panelling within the structure should also be retained.
4. It is also recognised that some compromise will need to be adopted in preparing any scheme for re-use. This is particularly the case in respect of generating re-use of the upper floor as the existing staircase provision is considered inadequate. Developing a scheme that delivers appropriate access and fire separation to the upper floor will be the key to unlocking the long-term sustainability of this building.

This long-term sustainable future arose in 2004 with an opportunity provided by the South East England Development Agency's (SEEDA) desire to fund the construction and operation of an enterprise gateway unit to help build and sustain a creative cluster in Medway, while also aiding graduate retention in the Medway towns, particularly from the University of Creative Arts Rochester Campus. The challenge for the Trust was first to persuade SEEDA that its Creative Industries Starter Unit for Medway should be in the historic dockyard and second that the Joiners' Shop would provide an ideal location for it.

Once agreement had been reached, SEEDA, as principal funder, undertook the role of lead partner and appointed both a development partner and a design team led by Bennetts Associates who specialised in sustainable approaches to development. The Trust was represented by Nigel Howard, its historic buildings manager. Key objectives for the project were to

- deliver the facilities required for a creative industries enterprise gateway;
- develop a scheme that respected the needs of the historic building and that would secure Scheduled Monument Consent;
- achieve BREEAM (Building Research Establishment Environmental Assessment Method) Very Good standards.

Recognising the challenge of achieving such a combination in the Joiners' Shop, Bennetts Associated worked closely with Baynes & Mitchell Architects who they had used to adapt a historic building elsewhere into their own offices. In 2007 SEEDA appointed Basepoint to take on the role of development partner and to manage the centre once completed. A project review led to Baynes & Mitchell taking on the role of lead architect and was the beginning of a long-term relationship between them and the Chatham Historic Dockyard Trust (CHDT/the Trust) that would result in

Joiners' Shop: Front elevation after adaptation, showing first-floor ribbon window and new external doors and draught lobby set within the entrance. The original sliding timber doors are fixed open.

[Chatham Historic Dockyard Trust]

Joiners' Shop: Interior view of the front of the ground floor 'building within a building', inserted with clear separation between it and the building's historic fabric.
[Chatham Historic Dockyard Trust/ Nebulo Strata]

their work, first, on the 1865 Armour Plate Shop, and more recently the Command of the Oceans/Ship beneath the Floor project, which was to become a finalist in the 2017 RIBA Stirling Prize.

Baynes & Mitchell adopted a 'building within a building' approach for the larger open spaces of the Joiners' Shop. On the ground floor a central core was created to house larger studio, exhibition or training spaces, with central 'tea' space, WCs, shower and plant room. A platform lift rated for both people and goods gave access to the first floor, where a similar central core structure provided some workspaces and support facilities. At this level a large open-plan work area, lit from an adjacent long ribbon window (one of the building's key features) provides an opportunity to read the historic building and its structure.

Overall, 47 units were provided, many created through the division of larger historic spaces with stud wall partitions, and wherever possible all such new elements, including the two central cores, were made to be independent of the historic structure and to be effectively reversible in the future. New insertions were expressed by the use of new materials, detailed in a contemporary manner, and use of different colour palettes. Opportunities were taken to highlight historic features discovered during the works – for example, a deep chamber with line shafting installed to drive early steam-powered machinery which is now lit beneath a glazed floor so all can see it.

BREEAM sustainable building certification brought its own challenges, particularly in the context of insulating a relatively lightweight roof structure. This was solved by the use of new hidden steel portal frames to reinforce historic trusses and roof beams to support the additional insulation load required.

Joiners' Shop: First floor kitchen unit – modern finishes and bright colours have been used to provide contrast to the historic building. [Chatham Historic Dockyard Trust/ Nebulo Strata]

The main historic staircase failed to meet guidance as it was too steep and without landings, while a secondary internal stairway was also totally inadequate, lacking appropriate fire protection, failing to lead directly to an external door and being in an inappropriate location. A fire engineering approach was used, with new external escapes erected at the rear of the building (carefully located to minimise visual impact), combined with the installation of a ground-floor fire suppression sprinkler system.

Together the project has created a light, bright and airy creative industries centre which achieved a BREEAM classification of 'Very Good'. The tenant starter unit offer is based on 'easy in' and 'easy out' terms that has been at the forefront of developing the historic dockyard as a creative industries cluster in the Thames Gateway Production corridor. Since opening in January 2009, the Joiners' Shop has seen very high levels of occupation and supported the launch of a number of highly successful companies including that of Dovetail Games, initially a start-up in the Joiners' Shop and now a major tenant in the dockyard's Fitted Rigging House.

Adaptation of No. 1 Smithery for national museum collections – one of three strategic museum partnerships

Over the past 25 years the Trust has developed three strategic museum partnerships that have resulted in the use of the historic dockyard's buildings by other museums and their collections. All add to the on-site visitor experience. Further, all bring additional benefits to the dockyard and wider Medway and North Kent community, for example through their own individual brand values and associations or the value of joint working and partnership. All provide uses for dockyard buildings as part of the Trust's strategy of 'preservation through reuse' and all deliver tangible and intangible value.

No. 1 Smithery: 'Honest' brickwork repairs to the courtyard north lodge clearly show evidence of previous subsidence.
[CHDT/VHH/James Brittain]

No. 1 Smithery: The outer wall of the Permanent Exhibition Gallery – stepped back from a group of historic forges carefully refitted following works to underpin the west wall to the right.
[CHDT/VHH/James Brittain]

The first two museum partnership projects fall within the simple adaptation or refurbishment group of reuse projects. These were:

- 'Lifeboat', 1996, a partnership with the Royal National Lifeboat Institution (RNLI) to display its historic lifeboat collection in No. 4 Slip (Scheduled Monument and Grade I Listed) through the simple insertion of a free-standing walkway to give access to more than 16 historic lifeboats and associated interpretation.
- 'The Big Store', 2008, large object storage on display in No. 3 Slip (Scheduled Monument and Grade I Listed) in partnership with the Royal Engineers Museum, Libraries and Archives through the use of an open-store approach with interventions to the building limited to the addition of two new metal stairs and passenger lift to provide visitor access to the building mezzanine and its iconic roof structure.

The third project, however, was on a very different scale – in size, complexity, development and outcomes. This was the £13 million project to adapt No. 1 Smithery (Scheduled Monument and Grade II* Listed), a 4,000 sq m, very dilapidated metal-working building on the English Heritage 'At Risk' Register, that occupied a prominent location at the heart of the historic dockyard, into a building fit for the storage and display of national museum collections.

In 2001, finding a use for No. 1 Smithery was the historic dockyard's most intransigent problem. At the same time, the National Maritime Museum (now Royal Museums Greenwich) faced the potential loss of one if its main collection stores; national museums were under pressure from government to expand their activities in the regions; and also under pressure to work together to develop shared solutions to such issues as collection storage. The Smithery project provided solutions and opportunities to address all.

The project survived an early setback following the failure of the scheme's first application for a Heritage Lottery Fund (HLF) grant. Initially conceived when the open-store model of 'storage on display' was at its height in the early years of the 21st century, the original concept was developed to bring together the maritime model collections of three national museums – Royal Museums Greenwich (RMG), Imperial War Museum (IWM) and Science Museum London. This would form the National Ship Model Collection Centre. Kent Architecture Centre led a competition on behalf of the partners for the appointment of an architect-led design consortium, which was won by a team led by van Heyningen & Haward Architects. The resultant scheme developed on a 'box within a box' concept and saw the installation of a number of two-storey buildings within the envelope of the historic building in order to provide accommodation for curtain-walled display structures capable of containing over 4,000 ship models.

By the time the first application for funding from HLF had been submitted, enthusiasm for storage-on-display schemes was waning and it was felt that the project had to deliver more outcomes with less visual impact on the building. This resulted in a complete rethink of the scheme by partners and the design team. At this time the Science Museum decided to withdraw from the scheme, and this proved helpful in designing a new two-museum solution involving fewer models.

No. I Smithery: Inside the National Maritime Museum store for large cased models. The corridor gives visitors the opportunity to see into the store, but also gives access for deliveries from the courtyard. [CHDT/VHH/James Brittain]

No. I Smithery: Treasures Gallery – display cases are sized to enable most models in the two collections to be displayed if required. [CHDT/VHH/James Brittain]

The changes implemented, although based on the concepts developed for the first scheme (box within a box and floor raised above 1,000-year flood level), were substantial. The scheme moved away from the storage-on-display approach, where most of the models were to be visible, to one that blended high-density 'closed' passive-environment stores with two high-quality exhibition spaces. One such space was developed as a gallery for display of objects from the two national museums' collections – with a Collections Research Area attached to both the gallery and the passive-environment stores. The other was fitted out to international security and environmental standards to function as a temporary exhibition gallery for the historic dockyard, where it has successfully staged a wide range of shows displaying material from

No. I Smithery: The first exhibition in the temporary exhibition gallery was of the Imperial War Museum's newly conserved Stanley Spencer's Shipbuilding on the Clyde series of paintings. It has proved to be a most versatile space.

[CHDT/VHH/James Brittain]

national and international museums and collections. Both gallery spaces were provided with full air conditioning to provide quality environmental conditions and museum-specification display cases.

The Smithery project tested a developing CHDT strategy for major projects – that of seeking to quantify risks before main contractors were appointed and took control of the site. This strategy of investing early to identify and mitigate risk has proved to be a highly effective tool in managing costs in all the Trust's later projects. In the context of the Smithery project, this involved letting two enabling contracts to resolve significant building contamination and structural integrity issues as part of a building emergency stabilisation contract agreed with HLF to be undertaken as part of the then stage 1 project development process. These enabled the Smithery to be cleared of asbestos residues (including about 500 tons of metal objects, tools and equipment, all assessed for their historic significance and for subsequent retention as part of the Trust's museum collections), and enabled the project's structural engineers to underpin the Smithery's west elevation, which was in increasing danger of imminent collapse.

Once the HLF's stage 2 pass had been secured and permission to start granted, a further enabling contract was let to undertake archaeological investigations necessary because of the extent of piling required to support the new passive-environment store buildings and exhibition spaces. This work led to the discovery of an extensive network of brick-built wind drains buried beneath the floor. Understanding their significance and importance took time and also led the structural engineers (Price & Myers) to redesign their piling plan to avoid damage and led to the piling element of the works being undertaken under both structural engineer and archaeologist supervision in advance of the appointment of the main contractor. This process of understanding and mitigating significant risk, primarily the risks of the 'unknown', played a major part in both programme and cost management, and avoided costly prolongation claims due to delays incurred while resolving them.

During construction, the project's main contractor entered into administration at a critical phase of the project, again testing inter-partner and design team relationships and reaffirming the impact of strong project direction from the lead partner, in this case the Trust's chief executive, Bill Ferris, and close working relationships with both national museums' directors, Roy Clare (RMG) and Sir Robert Crawford (IWM), as well as with the design team, project managers and HLF. A new contractor was appointed to complete the project, undertaking both the remaining elements of the main works as well as the fit-out of both stores and exhibition galleries. The Smithery opened to visitors in July 2010, only a few months later than planned, the first exhibition in the temporary gallery being one based on the IWM's Shipbuilding on the Clyde series of paintings by Stanley Spencer, curated by the then dockyard-based contemporary visual artist, Stephen Turner.

Although very different in scale, the success of all three museum partnerships was underpinned by common factors that resulted in successful delivery and ongoing partnerships. These were:

People
Investment of time in developing and maintaining interpersonal relationships, built on wider long-standing sector or regional museum partnerships and collaborations. From its inception in 1984, CHDT sought to play an active role in the wider maritime and industrial museum community, both nationally and internationally. Engagement with these organisations at a senior level played an instrumental role in all the Trust's strategic museum partnerships. People do business with people. Personal relationships matter.

The partnership between CHDT and the RNLI that led to 'Lifeboat' in 1996 was brokered through personal relationships developed through the UK Maritime Curators Group; that with the Royal Engineers Museum through joint programme activity with the Kent Medway Museum partnership and the Museums, Libraries and Archives Council (MLA) and the Renaissance South East museum hub in the years between 2002 and 2008. In addition, some ten years earlier, links with the three national museums (Imperial War Museum, National Maritime Museum and Science Museum) had been facilitated through the Trust's engagement with the work of the United Kingdom Maritime Collections Strategy group.

Partnerships of purpose
The success of all three strategic museum partnerships can also be attributed to the real benefits they delivered to each individual partner. Although these were often different for each partner, they all provided a solution to an immediate or long-term issue for those involved.

The 1996 lifeboat gallery secured a home for the RNLI's collection of historic lifeboats that had been displayed in an independent museum in Bristol's M Shed, which had closed several years previously, while providing the historic dockyard with a new maritime-related gallery. This provided a valued solution for the RNLI and offered the CHDT association with the RNLI brand.

No. 1 Smithery afforded solutions to individual issues facing each museum partner, and by working together enabled significant funding to be raised for the benefit of all. It also enabled the benefit of a placemaking impact by bringing national collections and branding to Medway and North Kent.

Planning and project direction
The Trust's experience of delivering complex partnership projects identifies the importance of taking a high-level approach to planning, project direction and project management. In all cases success can be traced to the continued engagement of all partners at senior levels (generally director/chief executive) and wider partner teams throughout the development and delivery period. Responsibility for maintaining inter-partner relationships cannot be delegated!
It also identified the importance of maintaining direct control over project delivery. Although professional and highly experienced project managers and design teams were employed, key decision-making processes – especially where these involved significant cost implications or major change – demanded formal partner sign-off. This proved essential to maintaining control of both costs and programme. Strict enforcement of ring-fenced fit-out budgets through change management systems protected them from reduction as a result of cost overruns elsewhere.

Sail and Colour Loft and Royal Dockyard Church:
Adaptation for university use

By 2010, completion of the Joiners' Shop and No. 1 Smithery projects had dealt with two of the Trust's larger and more difficult underutilised buildings, with the Trust's 2011–16 Corporate Plan identifying the Sail and Colour Loft and Fitted Rigging House as being high priorities for adaptation and reuse.

In 1984 the Trust took over an existing tenant in the Sail and Colour Loft (Zephyr Flags), who had been brought in by the Ministry of Defence in 1983 to secure the future of flag-making on site, supported by a five-year order book. The Trust utilised part of the ground floor and middle floor to provide a viewing gallery to enable visitors to watch flag making in action, but this closed following the demise of flag making at Chatham, and its story amalgamated into the 2002 Development Programme-funded Museum of the Royal Dockyard on the ground floor of the Fitted Rigging House. By then, part of the Sail and Colour Loft's ground floor had also been the subject of a simple refurbishment for use by a specialist architectural handrail design company, but over two-thirds of the building lay vacant.

In 2004 the Sail and Colour Loft (Scheduled Monument and Grade I Listed) was seen as being potentially very difficult to adapt because of its historical importance and associations; its physical layout with upper floors built as long, open loft spaces for the making of sails and flags; and

Sail and Colour Loft: First-floor
north still in use as a flag loft at the
time of dockyard closure.
[Chatham Historic Dockyard Trust]

its location behind Commissioners House garden effectively landlocking it within the historic dockyard's residential area.

The Trust's conservation plan identifies the building as being 'of exceptional significance (category A) as an important early eighteenth century naval storehouse and workshop that is now the sole surviving Sail Loft in any Royal Dockyard' and one with 'significant associations with ships of Pepys' navy and with key ships and events of the eighteenth and nineteenth centuries including the Victory and the Battle of Trafalgar'. Key associations having most impact on future use were the reused warship timbers that supported the upper sail loft floor – these showed signs of previous reuse, potentially in both other ships and buildings prior to insertion into the Sail and Colour Loft in the 1730s, suggesting them to be 17th century in origin – and the building's role during the major conflicts of the long 18th century, particularly in the context of *Victory*'s refit at Chatham prior to the Battle of Trafalgar.

In 2011, following a number of failed attempts to interest potential tenants in the building (including investigating potential options ranging from call centre/financial industry use to a major dance school), the Trust took the decision to relocate its own offices into the first floor as a trailblazer to prove that high-quality adaptation was possible without damaging the building's key historic attributes and importance and to encourage others to follow suit. Part of the works carried out (led by

Sail and Colour Loft: First-floor north adaptation for the Trust's offices seen shortly before completion. The mix of meeting rooms and individual and open-plan office areas carefully designed to provide long views through the space and emphasise historic fabric, especially the reused ships' timbers roof beams that had had a life at sea before the building was erected in the 1730s.

[Chatham Historic Dockyard Trust]

Sail and Colour Loft: Reuse of the upper floors was facilitated by the insertion of a new stair core with platform lift. The glass balustrades, seen here in the final stages of construction, were designed and installed by Handrail Design, one of the Trust's tenants based in the ground floor of the Sail and Colour Loft itself.

[Chatham Historic Dockyard Trust]

Nigel Howard, the Trust's historic buildings manager and in-house clerk of works/project manager) were designed to make the remainder of the building more suitable for reuse by inserting a central core within the building, with stairs and platform lift giving access to all floors, and in the process creating four new lettable areas. These works were financed by the Trust itself using its own development fund (established from the proceeds of some small residential development in 2004) with payback financed through the letting of spaces previously used as the Trust's offices.

The Trust's new offices occupied two-thirds of the building's middle floor and were carefully designed to ensure that long views through the length of the space remained through the provision of a large open-plan office and careful location of a few smaller offices and meeting rooms. Particular attention was paid to the installation of bespoke secondary glazing to each window, designed to maintain the character of each aperture, minimise visual impact both internally and externally, and maintain natural ventilation throughout.

The remainder of the first floor was let on a temporary basis to the University of Kent's Centre for Music and Fine Art as a student art studio. By then the university had an established presence in the historic dockyard, stemming from the adaptation of the central Clocktower Building as the Bridge Wardens' College in 1997. This in itself was an important milestone for tertiary education in the Medway towns, being the first physical university presence in Medway, funded by Rochester Bridge Trust in a particularly adroit piece of philanthropy that supported both the University of Kent's ambitions and the Trust's reuse of the site. Later, SEEDA were to enable the creation of a new university campus for Medway in HMS *Pembroke*, the former naval barracks adjacent to the historic dockyard, which now provides accommodation for the universities of Greenwich, Kent and Christ Church Canterbury.

Soon after the Trust had established its own presence in the Sail and Colour Loft and provided the necessary infrastructure to enable reuse of the remaining unoccupied areas of the building, the University of Kent sought space to provide facilities for a Medway outstation of its highly successful Business School. While the Sail and Colour Loft met many of their requirements, it could not accommodate an essential large lecture theatre capable of accommodating over 250 students at any one time. The solution was to be found through the adaptation of the adjacent Royal Dockyard Church (Scheduled Monument and Grade II* Listed), built in 1806 as a traditional-style Georgian chapel with an upper-floor gallery on three sides, to the design of Edward Holl, the Navy Board architect of the time.

Like the Sail and Colour Loft, the church posed many challenges that had to be resolved to the satisfaction of all parties (the Trust, English Heritage and the university) before it could be brought into the desired reuse. The Royal Dockyard Church had remained in use as a dockyard chapel until 1981 and had retained many of its internal fixtures and fittings, including original cast iron reeded columns supporting the first-floor gallery, itself complete with its original Georgian box pews. The ground floor retained late-Victorian pews, pulpit and organ, while both floors retained memorials to sailors, marines or ships lost over the years.

Royal Dockyard Church: View of
the ceiling after redecoration
using traditional hand-brushing
techniques.
[Chatham Historic Dockyard Trust]

Some religious iconography remained in place behind the altar. Above all, Holl's design had resulted in a beautiful, simple and symmetrical building that deserved utmost respect and a very delicate touch. It was for all these reasons that it had been retained by the Trust and used occasionally for its original purpose: an annual carol service and occasional services to commemorate significant events, for example the fiftieth anniversary of VE day. Such minimal use was thought unsustainable in the long term, but conversion to a university lecture theatre was seen as being for the good of the building, provided it could be achieved with minimal intervention.

Royal Dockyard Church: The
rebuilt original entrance steps with
new Portland stone access ramp
inserted behind.
[Chatham Historic Dockyard Trust]

Adaptation of both Sail and Colour Loft and Royal Dockyard Church for use by the university was the result of very close collaboration between the Trust, the university and the university's architects, Hazel McCormack Young. The works in the Sail and Colour Loft built on the approach already adopted by the Trust and saw the insertion of administrative offices on the ground floor south of the new central core, academic offices above them on the first floor, and a suite of seminar rooms on the upper floor delivered in a manner that retained long views through the building on the western elevation that also retained views over Commissioners House and its garden.

The Royal Dockyard Church was more complex. The Trust undertook works to extend and deepen the church's small crypt to enable new WC facilities to be inserted in the building, accessed by an original staircase. These works required underpinning of the ground-floor support beams to accommodate the reduced level required for the WC area and increased loads on the floor above. Two disabled WCs were installed on the ground floor in what had been the original vestry. Externally, the Portland stone steps to the main entrance were brought forward from the front of the building to provide sufficient space to enable a new Portland stone ramp to be inserted to provide disabled access. Here, as indeed everywhere, success was the direct result of close attention to detail, use of specialist contractors and, above all, detailed briefing of their workforce to enable all involved in the project to understand the Trust's objectives. This is well illustrated by the internal decoration works undertaken to walls and ceiling where the paint was applied traditionally using brushes rather than more modern rollers or spray. The result speaks for itself.

Internal adaptation works were led by Hazel McCormack Young. The ground-floor late-Victorian pews were removed after long discussion with English Heritage, to be replaced with a modern retractable 'bleacher' seating system. Here, great importance was placed on reversibility, and although the pews were not retained, the retractable seating was split into two separate banks, both on wheels to enable them to be separated and rolled back beneath the rear gallery and the original view from the entrance to the altar revealed. The original Georgian box pews were retained on the balcony, with the rear elevation and part of both sides used to provide additional seating. Gallery balustrades were of insufficient height to meet current regulations and were extended by discreet glazed panels that are barely visible from below. A new and entirely reversible projection booth was added above some of the rear balcony box pews and equally discreet LED lighting added to enable students working in these areas to have sufficient light.

Memorial plaques were covered by demountable acoustic panels and the religious iconography behind the altar area covered by full-height electrically operated curtains. A large, powered screen drops down in front of the curtains for presentations, and a sophisticated audio and presentation system was installed to meet university requirements.

The adaptation of the church proved most successful, enabling the character of Holl's original building to be retained while meeting the Business School's requirements for a modern state-of-the-art lecture theatre. Equally important, the building can still be used for the Trust's annual carol service, as the Trust retained limited use of the church

Royal Dockyard Church: Internal view of the completed lecture theatre (with retractable 'bleacher' seating extended); the glazed gallery ballustrade extensions are barely visible and the new projection booth is completely reversible.

[Chatham Historic Dockyard Trust]

by agreement with the university as part of its lease arrangements. The audio-visual screen lifted up and curtains drawn back enables the remaining religious iconography to be revealed with little effort. Guests, however, now have the benefit of seating infinitely more comfortable than the previous Victorian pews!

The Ship beneath the Floor and Command of the Oceans

In 1989–90 the Trust tackled its first major restoration project (the pre-existing 1985–7 Ropery project having been inherited from the Ministry of Defence). This was the repair and preservation of the Mast Houses and Mould Loft (Scheduled Monument and Grade I Listed) – an iconic timber-framed and -clad building erected in 1753–5 to provide accommodation for the yard's mast makers. During construction, a Mould Loft was built above where it is believed the lines of the *Victory* were laid down (scribed into the floor) a few years later. By 1984 both it and the adjacent Wheelwrights' Shop (Scheduled Monument and Grade II* Listed) had been overclad in metal sheeting and had had their roofs replaced with asbestos cement sheets. Internally, a metre-high concrete platform had been cast in the main body of the Mast Houses and Mould Loft in the aftermath of 1953 east-coast flooding, leading to severe rot in many of the building's timber posts – themselves reused warship timbers from ships at sea during the first half of the 18th century.

The 1989 works were overseen by Martin Caroe Architects and followed a traditional approach to restoration. The metal cladding was removed, timber posts and timber cladding repaired or renewed with like-for-like materials, and the asbestos sheeting replaced with hand-made Kent peg tiles. The industrial nature of the building was reinforced by decisions not to introduce insulation or even sarking felt beneath the tiles on the single-storey Mast Houses – a decision which was to prove costly in the future with high energy costs being expended in often futile attempts to keep staff and visitors warm in winter months. Wooden Walls, the Trust's first major museum gallery, was inserted into the building, bringing to life the story of wooden warship construction at Chatham through a reconstruction of the dockyard of 1758.

At the same time, the easternmost of the Wheelwrights' Shop's three bays was adapted for catering use to become the Trust's principal visitor catering offer. In 1995 the Trust embarked on a programme of works funded by a grant from English Heritage to repair further historic buildings on site to enable them to be brought into commercial reuse. These included the remaining two bays of the Wheelwrights' Shop, which had been used by a joinery firm since 1984. They were relocated to the Brunel sawmills. The building's roof was renewed with peg tiles, metal sheeting stripped off external walls, and exposed timber planking repaired and redecorated. A programme of archaeological investigation was also launched to explore the history and use of up to five different levels of timber floors that had been built over many years within the building as a precursor to their removal and replacement with a new floor more suitable for adaptation for reuse.

This project, led by Oxford Archaeology, made an astonishing discovery – beneath all these different floors they found a floor comprised of ships' side planking, supported on over 200 pieces of a wooden warship's frame. Further investigation by the Scottish Institute of Marine Studies concluded that the timbers and planking came from the same vessel and the find was described as being the 'single most important warship find in northern waters since that of the *Mary Rose*'. With it the opportunity for a 'quick-win' commercial reuse of the building evaporated, and the Trust embarked on a 20-year quest to find out more about the ship itself and find a solution both to its long-term preservation and a future use for the building. A temporary viewing gallery was inserted at the south end of the Wheelwrights' Shop middle bay to enable limited visitor access to the find.

By 2010, archaeological and historical research had concluded that the ship beneath the floor was the remains of a single ship, the second-rate ship of the line *Namur*, launched at Chatham in 1756 and broken up at Chatham in 1833–4 after an illustrious career during which she had taken part in nine fleet actions over three worldwide wars and had associations with a wide range of significant people, including Olaudah Equiano, a key figure in the fight to abolish the slave trade, Jane Austen's naval brother, Captain Charles Austen, as well as major naval figures of the time.

By 2010 the Trust had also reached the conclusion that it needed to reorganise its core museum historical galleries (which had seen the Age of Sail story split between the 1990 Wooden Walls gallery and the 2004 Museum of the Royal Dockyard in the Fitted Rigging House at opposite ends of the site to each other), and in the process undertake major energy efficiency and insulation works to the Mast Houses and Mould Loft to reduce running costs and energy wastage. An initial study by architects ADP and designers Equal proposed a strategy for doing so which involved

Command of the Oceans: External landscaping redefined the site of the 1697 south mast pond and revealed the entrance to Marc Brunel's sawmill timber canal.
[Chatham Historic Dockyard Trust]

a new single-storey structure between both Mast Houses and Mould Loft and Wheelwrights' Shop, extending out to the south mast pond to provide a new and more visible entrance to the historic dockyard, and reworked galleries within the Mast Houses and Mould Loft which would include selected timbers from the find, with the rest preserved *in situ*.

An HLF Stage 1 bid was made in 2011 based on the ADP/Equal study. This was not successful, feedback following the failure leading the Trust to undertake a major re-appraisal of the project including aims, objectives, scope and consultation. The result was a very different proposal focused on developing a sense of arrival to the historic dockyard. The context for this was a potential bid for World Heritage status. The new project also encompassed landscape improvements to the 12-acre site to the north of the buildings that included the historic dockyard's two oldest monuments, the 1696 and 1702 mast ponds. The earlier gallery reorganisation scheme was broken into separate phases, with work to renew the Museum of the Royal Dockyard as Steam, Steel and Submarines, a smaller gallery focusing on the 19th- and 20th-century story of the site to be undertaken and funded separately.

Prior to submission of the first HLF application, the Trust had already begun procurement through European Union Public Procurement Procedures advertised in the Official Journal of the European Union of an architect-led design team. Expressions of interest were whittled down to a small number of teams invited to pitch. Most schemes presented shared a common approach of inserting a new single-storey structure into the gap between the Mast Houses and Mould Loft of varying sizes and impact, enabling the historic ship timbers to be viewed from above – either through fully or partially glazed floors or walkways that connected the new structure with the Wheelwrights' restaurant beyond. One scheme, however, that put forward by Baynes & Mitchell (who had led the adaptation of the Joiners' Shop), was very different, very original and inspired.

Rather than viewing the timbers from above, Baynes & Mitchell proposed inserting a two-storey building in the gap between the two monuments, with the lower floor excavated below ground level and a new raised floor inserted above the timbers to create sufficient space for a new and atmospheric viewing gallery below a 'free to enter' area before the ticketing desk with initial interpretation, catering and retail areas. Their new structure was designed to fit entirely within the gap to provide a raised new visitor entrance that was highly visible by the use of modern materials to differentiate it from both adjacent historic buildings, but not intrusive. By careful use of differing levels between and within the two buildings their proposals allowed access to most areas by compliant ramps.

Command of the Oceans: Internal view of Baynes & Mitchell's elegant cross-laminated timber-framed roof to the new entrance bay. Hidden from site above is an array of photo-voltaic panels.
[Chatham Historic Dockyard Trust/ Baynes & Mitchell]

Command of the Oceans: View across the historic dockyard from the new entrance bay. For the first time visitors could see into the heart of the historic dockyard before paying to visit.
[Chatham Historic Dockyard Trust]

A key decision taken by the Trust at this time was to delay procurement of the exhibition design team until after that of the architectural team, enabling the lead architect, Alan Mitchell, to take part in the process that led to the appointment of Land Design Studios (who had previously worked on the Smithery project). This proved highly effective and ensured that both architects and designers complemented each other's approaches and resulted in excellent coordination between the two.

Funding for the project was complex, matching an HLF grant with funding derived from other sources, including SEEDA. This was in relationship to the two mast ponds to the north, which, while owned by the Trust, were a significant element of a wider development site owned by SEEDA on either side. The historic landscape improvement works undertaken as part of the Command of the Oceans project were seen as critical to attracting appropriate development of those potential sites. The SEEDA funding element was time limited by the Treasury, giving little overlap with the programme for securing permission to start from HLF. This resulted in two separate contracts being awarded – one for the external works and one for those to the buildings.

As in previous projects, the Trust's board and executive maintained close oversight and engagement, with a board subcommittee established. Bill Ferris, as CEO, took the role of project director, Richard Holdsworth as client project lead and Nigel Howard as client project manager and Trust clerk of works, ensuring close coordination between Trust, design team, project manager (Stephen Prowse) and cost consultant (Bob Dollin), both appointed directly through Artelia UK, Project Management and Cost Consultants. The Trust's rigorous change control procedures were applied once the detailed design had been 'fixed', with both architect and exhibition design teams constantly challenged to compensate for any cost increases by finding equivalent savings elsewhere within their own areas of activity. Fit-out budgets were ring fenced and indeed increased where necessary during the lifetime of the project.

The value of this approach to management of the project and stakeholder relationships was again demonstrated when the main contractor, FWA Restoration Ltd entered administration following failure of the wider FWA Group company. This occurred at a critical stage of construction, with the main concrete work only part complete. The Trust's executive, project manager and cost consultant's previous experience of this situation (No. 1 Smithery project) led to immediate action being taken to determine the contract and take direct control of the site. To prevent a major break in construction, the concrete subcontractor was directly employed by the Trust to complete those works and the contractor that was in the process of completing the University of Kent's works to the Sail and Colour Loft taken on through a process of negotiation with key funders in a manner which kept most of FWA's subcontractors engaged. Further costs inevitably occurred, but, again, the importance of requiring contractors to take out bonds to cover such circumstances reduced liability to the Trust and HLF. As a result, the project was completed and opened only two months later than planned, in May 2016.

A finalist in the RIBA's prestigious Stirling Prize, details of the architecture and outcomes are well documented elsewhere and can be seen in the photographs included here. The result was outstanding and

a real tribute to Baynes & Mitchell's original design concept and the contribution that the entire design team made in terms of attention to detail. This extended from board-marked concrete, to the ingenious system devised by the project structural engineers, Price & Myers, for supporting the new floor over the ships' timbers without visible means of support, and to exhibition design, where an innovative approach to storytelling through five interlinked audio-visuals with a well-known presenter seen on screen (rather than just through voice-over) has made a complex story easily understood. The Trust had secured a solution for the long-term preservation of the ship-beneath-the-floor archaeological site and, in the process, delivered a high-quality main visitor entrance and sense of arrival appropriate for a world-class heritage location.

Command of the Oceans: The Ship Beneath the Floor, the final gallery allows visitors to see the timbers of the Chatham-built second-rate 90-gun ship *Namur* preserved *in situ* in the Wheelwrights' shop beneath a new floor. Price and Myers' structural solution enabled the floor to be suspended across both bays of the building without visible means of support.
[Chatham Historic Dockyard Trust/ Rikard Osterlund]

Conclusions

All four projects outlined above chart the Trust's progress in moving from simple refurbishment-based adaptations for reuse, be it commercial or museum, to much more sophisticated models that clearly demonstrate what can be achieved in historic buildings and structures in an appropriate and sympathetic manner.

All share a number of common success factors:

- Close and ongoing engagement by the Trust's executive team in managing both delivery and stakeholder (particularly funder) relationships.
- Investment in in-house knowledge and expertise – particularly the role of the Trust's historic buildings specialist as internal clerk of works in order to maintain a daily watching brief over works as they progressed.
- Direct appointment of key external project manager and cost consultant roles, rather than being appointments of lead architects or others engaged in project delivery.
- Developing and implementing rigorous change control procedures.
- Early de-risking of projects wherever possible through enabling works to investigate hidden archaeology or other factors, for example contamination, at early stages of project development and before appointment of the main contractor.
- Early identification of key elements of the fabric not only to be preserved, but to be kept clearly visible, and a willingness to adapt design approaches to celebrate features discovered along the way.
- Encouraging attention to detail by the whole project team from developing an early shared understanding of the importance of the historic building through to educating and enthusing contractors and their skilled tradesmen in the role they can play through their workmanship.

Above all, the Trust remained undeterred by funding setbacks, accepting that sometimes it takes time!

Contributors

Jonathan Coad
Jonathan Coad is the leading authority on the history of Britain's Royal dockyards and naval bases. His magnum opus, *Support for the Fleet: Architecture and Engineering of the Royal Navy's Bases 1700–1914*, published by English Heritage in 2013, is the definitive history. As an inspector of ancient monuments, with responsibilities in East Anglia and later South East England, he worked with the Ministry of Defence to secure a future for the historic dockyard at Chatham. In 1997 he evaluated for UNESCO the Swedish naval base at Karlskrona, leading to its inscription on the World Heritage list. He is a vice president of the Society for Nautical Research, a fellow of the Society of Antiquaries, and has been president of the Royal Archaeological Institute.

Neil Cossons
Sir Neil Cossons OBE was for 12 years the first director of the Ironbridge Gorge Museum Trust in Shropshire, before being appointed director of the National Maritime Museum, Greenwich. Here, in the mid-1980s, he was closely involved, mainly with Harry Deakin, director of planning for Kent County Council, in the moves to set up the Chatham Historic Dockyard Trust. After 14 years as director of the Science Museum London, he retired in 2000 and was appointed chairman of English Heritage, a post he held for seven years. As the result of a lifetime's engagement with industrial history and archaeology and conservation, he has advised governments, museums and conservation agencies in Britain and overseas, most notably in France, Japan, New Zealand and the United States.

Richard Holdsworth
Richard Holdsworth MBE studied history at the University of Leeds before beginning a career in museums and heritage in 1979. Following appointments with Merseyside County Museums and the Imperial War Museum, he joined Chatham Historic Dockyard Trust in 1985 as the site's first curator. Now director of heritage, public engagement and learning, he is responsible for the delivery of the Trust's educational and charitable purposes, including care of the Trust's historic ships and wider collections, as well as the community engagement and volunteering, learning and visitor experience teams. In 2009 he was awarded an MBE for services to heritage in Kent.

Paul Hudson
Paul Hudson is a planner and economic development specialist. He has worked for local, regional and central government, and development agencies. In that capacity he has been involved in the evolution of Chatham Dockyard from its closure in 1984, both in the creation of the Historic Dockyard Trust and as a current member of its board. He

had responsibilities in the early 2000s for the development of Chatham Maritime. His interest in heritage-based regeneration was greatly expanded as chairman of the Heritage Lottery Fund South East for six years, and as a long-standing member of the Chapter of Rochester Cathedral. Since retiring as the government's chief planner he has taken on a wide variety of infrastructure planning cases and projects nationally, and serves as a trustee and director of several arts and development schemes, most notably in Folkestone.

Paul Jardine

Paul Jardine is the managing director of Jura Consultants. The practice was founded in 1997 and is one of the leading management consultancies operating in the heritage sector. He is an accountant, an economist and an MBA, and has applied these skills to the heritage sector for over 30 years. He is currently deputy chair of Edinburgh World Heritage Trust, the independent charity that aims to ensure the city's World Heritage status benefits everyone. Treasurer of the Aperture Trust and a board member of the Tweed Forum, Paul is a visiting lecturer at University College London, where he contributes to the MSc in Sustainable Heritage.

Andrew Lambert

Andrew Lambert is the Laughton Professor of Naval History in the Department of War Studies at King's College London. One of Britain's most eminent historians, he has written prolifically on maritime matters, and is recognised internationally for his work on issues of military policy, security and deterrence, and crisis management. In 2018 he was awarded the prestigious Gilder Lehrman award for his book *Seapower States: Maritime Culture, Continental Empires and the Conflict that Made the Modern World* (Yale University Press, 2019). He is a fellow of the Royal Historical Society and was appointed a fellow of King's College London in 2020.

Index

Page numbers in **bold** refer to illustrations.